ALASKA SH*T HAPPENS!

AMUSING STORIES AND OBSERVATIONS FROM ALASKA'S OUTDOORS

by Rick Rydell

Library of Congress Control Number: 2007904778
ISBN# 9780979753305

Second Printing February 2008
10 9 8 7 6 5 4 3 2

Printed in the United States of America

Edited by: Justin Stiefel
Illustrations: Mike Ortega
Photographs: Author's personal collection
Book Design: Vered R. Mares, Todd Communications

This book was typeset in 13 point Bookman Old Style, that's 3 more than 10.

Published by:
IT HAPPENS PUBLISHING
808 S. Bailey, Suite 101
Palmer, Alaska 99645
www.650keni.com

Distributed exclusively by:
Todd Communications
611 E. 12th Ave.
Anchorage, Alaska 99501 U.S.A.
Tel. (907) 274-8633 (TODD)
Fax. (907) 929-5550
e-mail: sales@toddcom.com
with offices in Ketchikan, Juneau, Fairbanks & Nome, Alaska

Contents

1. Chumming For Bears 9

2. The Hunt 23

3. Trust Your Scope 31

4. River Halibut 41

5. Grouse Netting 49

6. Shark 59

7. Black Bear 67

8. Forget Your Gun 77

9. Chinook 89

10. Grizzly Bear 99

11. December Deer..111

12. "Save Him!" They Say 131

13. The Sound of Completion and Advil! 143

14. More, Bigger, Better Than You 161

15. While You Still Can 179

16. Check That Scope Before You Shoot 193

17. A Land of World Records 205

Forward

Rick Rydell is a very unusual man. As a morning radio personality in Anchorage, Alaska, his public persona is that of an unabashed redneck. He takes a rather perverse pride in it. He is also the most ardent and accomplished outdoorsman I know.

Name an Alaskan animal, Rick has shot it and likely has eaten it. He's not a gourmet chef, so most of them get made into sausage or hamburger. Dinner at Rick's is likely to include Hamburger Helper somewhere on the menu. For the few animals he has not shot and devoured, he is undoubtedly plotting right now.

For years, until advancing age played some tricks with his eyesight, he eschewed using a scope on his rifle. "For woosies", he would say. Implicit in that statement is the fact that Rick ain't no "woosie."

He bought a few traps and snares, found a wild place a little south of town, and spread 'em around. Don't think he ever caught much, but whatever it was, I'm pretty sure he ground it into hamburger and ate it.

As a fisherman, Rick is unsurpassed. He is a registered guide and hangs out with guides, learning what they know. And he practices.

In Alaska, almost anybody can catch a fish. But Rick catches more, bigger and more often. He is amazing. I've been fishing for fifty years, but I learn more from watching this young fella than I've learned in that whole time.

Best of all, Rick is the ultimate companion on any outdoor adventure. For instance, he will know more ways to set up a camp than you ever thought of. Some easier, most harder, but all interesting. He is easy-going, full of humor and totally at ease in the outdoors. The kind of guy you just like to be with. And, as you're about to learn, he is a consummate story teller. In "Alaska Happens", you get to know Rick pretty well.

There's not a made-up, or wildly exaggerated story here. Rick wouldn't do that. He wouldn't have to.

Jack Frost

Longtime Alaskan, Former Executive director of the Iditarod Sled dog race, two time candidate for Mayor of Anchorage, Broadcaster, Owner of Frost and Friends Advertising Agency.

Dedication

As a single father, every night I told my two sons a bedtime story. Sometimes I told them the stories you are about to read. One night, during a recital of "Chumming for Bears," my six-year-old stopped me and said, "Daddy, why don't you write your greatest adventures down and put pictures with them so we can read them to our kids when we become daddies?"

So I dedicate this book to my unborn grandchildren because their fathers had the foresight to plan for them. I hope my grandchildren realize what great dads they have; I can already see what wonderful men they will become.

A message to my grandkids:
> *Love your fathers. You are blessed*
> *to be raised by them. For they are*
> *to me, as I know you are to them,*
> *the inspirations for life itself!*

A message to my sons:
> *You asked me to write my greatest*
> *adventures, so here are some of*
> *them. I have to tell you, though,*
> *they are not my greatest adventure.*
> *My greatest adventure, by far, has*
> *been being your Dad.*

The morning after, it still looked weird

Chumming for Bears

We'd made the same trip just two nights before. Same boat, same creek, same driver, same guns and the same people. But that's where the similarity ended. The first trip didn't include a dead moose, hypothermia, engine problems, sleep deprivation or a plethora of voracious brown bears at close range.

I really didn't expect to see a moose. We had the "big moose hunt" planned the next day. This was a Saturday-night-just-for-the-hell-of-it trip. Oh, yes I took my rifle, but that was just out of habit. When you spend a lot of time beating around Bush Alaska you learn to always take your gun. People who don't pretty much qualify for wearing a badge marked *"Damned Fool."* Still, I was sure I wouldn't need it.

Funny how two rounds fired from one rifle can change the ambience of an after work boat ride and turn a beautiful wilderness creek into a pretty spooky place.

We were working an environmental construction job in King Salmon, Alaska. We were cleaning and rebuilding an old air force dump site called South Barrel Bluff. It didn't pain any of us that the Bluff just happened to be next to King Salmon Creek. This creek became our personal fishing grounds for the summer. It was full of kings, chum, pinks and silvers, not to mention rainbows, Dollys, and grayling.

Fishing slowed down by September. The bite of fall was in the air and we wanted to go on a boat ride to enjoy the season. Our plan was simple - get off work at 6:00 p.m., step into our skiff at 6:03. I call it a skiff, but the locals referred to it as our aluminum barge. It was a 22-foot flat-bottomed construction boat with a landing craft front end and an electric boom and winch on board. This metallic monstrosity was powered by a 460 V-8 that launched it out of the hole in just under a nano-second.

OK, maybe I've exaggerated a bit, but when guys talk about over-powered toys like our rocket sled, it's difficult to not want to scratch yourself, shotgun a beer, and see who can belch the loudest. We doubled our already overflowing shot of testosterone by packing two Ruger Super Redhawk .44 magnums, a .300 Winchester magnum, a .338 Winchester magnum, and enough hunting and skinning knives to sink any lesser water craft. We were men of the wilderness and ready for anything.

We left the dock, donned in rain-gear and hip boots, and headed down stream on the Naknek River. John Smithson was the construction site superintendent, Bryon Yocum and I operated heavy equipment. Smithson and I each had valid moose tags and planned on using them the next day during our "big hunt." We hit the confluence with King Salmon Creek at exactly 6:15 p.m. I know it was 6:15 p.m. when we entered the creek because Smithson, who was driving, turned to me and said, "Remember the time, 6:15 exactly." I remembered.

King Salmon Creek is generally only a foot in depth, with a few deeper spots when it bends. Like most creeks in the region, King Salmon Creek twists and turns like mad. We were on step to avoid hitting any shallow spots. I should change that to "try to" avoid hitting any shallow spots. It's tough when you're fighting a major bout of motion sickness from the tossing and turning of the boat not unlike the motion of the "Zipper" at the state fair. After an hour and fifteen minutes of the nearly nauseating high speed zigzagging, we stopped. We must have traveled at least 20 river miles upstream, but only as a "drunk" crow flies.

We decided, since most of the creek now was not as wide as our boat was long, it was probably a good time to turn around. We found a wide spot and changed direction. Heading back seemed to be a bit more relaxing, mainly, I think, because we had somewhat of a recollection of where the sweepers (overhanging trees) and boat-sinking rocks were because we ran into and bounced off of every single one on the way up.

Traveling downstream always seems to go a bit slower than traveling upstream, at least it feels that way, because the water is flowing in the same direction you are. After traveling about five minutes downstream, we began to enter a bend in the creek and Bryon began pointing dramatically to the right. Three moose climbed majestically out of the water.

As the boat came to rest against the far shore, I dove for my rifle. I pulled it from the case while the three moose had all stopped, just staring at us. I'm sure they were confused on just what this gargantuan silver aquatic animal was. I raised my .338 magnum. It was a long shot, maybe as far as forty feet. In the 3x9 Leupold, set on 3x, I found the biggest set of antlers, set the cross hairs and squeezed the trigger. BOOM!! The 44-inch bull with three brow tines on the left and four on the right went down.

Instinctively, I jacked another 250 grain slug into the chamber as I lowered the rifle from my shoulder. As I looked toward the downed bull, there was another standing broadside! I glanced at Smithson. He was fumbling around the bottom of the boat for his rifle. I yelled "here" as I tossed my Winchester in his direction. He caught it and drew it to his shoulder in one fluid motion. BOOM!! His 32-inch bull went down just as the third one decided to show us its heels.

Two shots, two downed moose, not bad for a joy-ride. Out of the boat we climbed to finish them off with matching .44s. We paused for a couple of choice pictures then gutted the animals and prepared them for transport.

We shot the animals in a big, horseshoe bend and they had fallen across the frog (the inside of the horseshoe) only twenty feet from the water. What great luck! We didn't have to haul them out on our backs. Smithson moved the boat into position while Bryon lowered the bow of the boat. Using the boom and winch we yarded-'em into the boat whole. Being a construction stiff has some advantages. By 8:30 we had them both gutted and aboard.

We started downstream totally convinced that we were absolutely, unequivocally the greatest hunters that ever graced the face of the earth, quite possibly the universe. We were bad and we knew it. Oddly enough we didn't feel so confidently skilled as sailors, because now with an extra two thousand pounds of weight, we couldn't get the boat up on step.

About five minutes later we clogged the jet intake with grass. First we tried reverse to blow it out. Then we tried the scrape method, to no avail. Finally we shut the engine off to stop the suction. We reached down and pulled out enough grass to keep an entire herd of Angus happy. Now with the jet-intake cleared of any and all obstruction, we were ready to cruise back to camp to claim our rightful title: heroes! Such would not be the case, however, as I tried to start the engine. NOTHING.

Apparently, when we used the winch and boom, it drained the battery. So much for cruising back to camp, we were obviously in for a long night, though none of us knew just how long at this point.

It was now 9:15 p.m., I know it was exactly 9:15 because Smithson looked at his watch and said, "We're dead in the water at 9:15. Remember the time." I remembered.

Boats draw a lot more water drifting than when they're traveling at a high rate of speed, so we figured we stood a much better chance of actually floating out of there if we stayed in the channel. Bryon grabbed a 2 x 4 and took up position on the bow while Smithson took up the stern. For a while I fancied them to be gondoliers as I floated along the waterways of Venice, sitting on the neck of a moose humming an Italian aria to myself.

The thoughts of Venice quickly dissipated as darkness enveloped us at 9:30. In late summer in Alaska darkness comes upon you slowly, lulling you into a false sense of confidence in your surroundings, until all of a sudden it is dark and you wonder where it came from. And in rural Alaska the darkness is total and all-encompassing. There is no ambient light, no glow on the horizon from a city, or factory, or highway, or neighborhood. There is nothing. Just blackness in every direction, to the point where you wonder if you have entered a very deep cave where daylight has never been seen.

I think it was about 10:10 when the first brown bear began walking the shore next to us. I'm sure to him and all his sharp-fanged, long-clawed carnivorous cousins that gave a social call to our boat that night, we seemed like a floating all-you-can-eat buffet.

Sometimes you could actually smell them, that stench of dead, rotten, carrion. Sometimes you could see their beady little red eyes looking at you from the bank. Sometimes you could hear the grass rustling four feet away from you, as something large was moving through it, shadowing your every turn. There were times when there were bears walking with us on both sides of the creek.

I'd really like to emphasize the word is 'creek.' It is not an ocean, lake, or even small river. It is a creek. Webster defines creek as follows: "'creek' \ 'krek, krik\ noun (1) trickle of water, barely a trickle (2) not enough damn water to keep a hungry brown bear from chewing your ass off."

At one point I was in the front of the boat with Bryon and we saw something black moving in the creek about 60 yards downstream. I told Smithson, who was in the stern, to look, too. He had a hard time seeing it until "Yogi" turned to look at us. That's when his eyes gathered enough light to shine red, like blood. We all felt a chill run down our backs. We drifted directly at him until we were about 20 yards away when, thank God, he ran out of the water and into the bushes.

If a bear wanted to walk to our boat, two steps from shore he'd be there. He probably wouldn't get wet above the knees. The creek was just not that deep, but we were up it with only 2 X 4s!

Did I mention the boat was sinking too? At the rear of the boat, slightly above the waterline, was a scupper on either side. A scupper is a hole in the freeboard that is usually just above the water level so that water can flow off the deck. With a ton of fresh raw meat on board these scuppers were now below the waterline, letting water in the boat. Since Smithson and Yocum were busy with their navigation responsibilities I took it upon myself to try and deal with the growing aquifer in the bottom of the boat. I plugged the holes as best I could and began bailing. While I couldn't plug the holes fully, it did seem to make it possible for me to stay a bit ahead of the incoming water.

As I bailed I noticed the water that was coming in was washing onto the fresh moose carcasses. As I poured bucket load after bucket load back into the creek, I realized this water was black with blood and full of eau de moose, and gave off a bear's favorite scent. It dawned on me that we were now chumming for brownies. Funny how minutes seem like hours when you're drifting through the savage wilderness in absolute blackness followed by ravenous bruins of humungous proportions.

The sweepers were part of the unexpected fun, too. I say unexpected because during the day or even in periods of lower light you could see them coming. But for us, as the darkness intensified, they had become something of a Russian roulette game when we sat anywhere near the side rail. At one point Smithson quickly bowed his head toward me. My eldest son was taking karate so I saw it as a sign of respect. I began to smile until I realized he bowed to escape a total facial reconstruction by the tree that apparently just barely missed my head. There are some advantages of being only 5'10".

The sweeper decided to attach itself to our port side where it dragged along with us for about an hour. We came to terms with it being there by convincing ourselves that we may need the firewood. The creek was fully lined with trees and logs were everywhere. Just ask any one of the hundreds of thousands of beavers who made this creek their home.

Oh yeah, the beavers! Did they ever add a bit of color to the trip? Let me explain a cute little personality trait beavers have, for those of you who don't spend a lot of time around them. When beaver's are in the water (which is most of the time) and they get alarmed, they slap the water with their wide flat tail and dive. While this slap is very interesting and even fun for most humans to hear during the day when the sun is shining and the birds are singing, it's more like the blast of a shotgun for drifters on a stream in the dead silence late at night in the wilderness.

Couple the piercing decibels shattering the stillness with the anxiety built up after all the big old fat hairy grizzly bears stalking us down the stream and I think you can see the entertainment value of a few dozen beavers. Suffice it to say more than one of the rodents were so put off by our presence that they "blasted" us with their particular brand of shotgun, making for a less than enjoyable experience. In fact, though I didn't check, Bryon, who was always in the front of the boat, therefore closest to the "slap", probably was in dire need of new underwear.

I doubt that this creek could be drifted without running aground at least once. We did the best we could to exceed that and I'm proud to say we were successful. We bounced off at least ten rocks, high centered on one for about twenty minutes, and ran up on gravel bars three times.

I think it was about 12:30 a.m. when we were pushing the boat off a gravel bar. Finally after a good half-hour of rocking, the front end I was pulling began to swing into deeper water.

I, with my keen observational skills, recognized that the cold sensation slowly climbing my leg was actually water rising inside my hip-waders. I took this as a sign to leap into the now freed boat.

As I jumped, my rain gear snagged on a wing nut leaving me clutching the side rail like a desperate man about to be swept under a dead boat floating down a wilderness creek in the middle of Alaska. This, of course, pretty much described my situation. My partners - Smithson, Bryon and God Himself - had presence of mind enough to grab me and pull me in the boat.

I could have been fighting hypothermia for the rest of the trip but thanks to the amount of water that had entered the boat in the last forty minutes, I had plenty of bailing exercise ahead to keep warm.

We finally reached our job site at 2:15 a.m. I knew the exact time for the same reasons as before. When he said it, I remembered. I hopped out of the boat as the other two tied it off. Up on top of the bluff was the Kobelco excavator I had been operating most of the summer. I walked it down the slope until I was next to the creek and lowered the bucket down to the boat. The guys tied the moose to it and I lifted both trophies out of the boat. We let them hang with the bottoms of their hooves about ten feet off the ground so the bears couldn't use them as a piñata.

It was 4 a.m. before we finished our celebratory beverage beers, and headed off to la la land to dream of something boring and mundane.

Rydell and Smithson right before the engine died

The developed trail where it still seems safe

The Hunt

The cold bite of fall hung in the air as the beast clawed his way through the primeval forest. The creature knew of my presence for at least 20 minutes. Of course he had known, this place we call wilderness, he and his kind have called home for thousands of years. What seems wild and bestial to us is a living room and kitchen to him. Day in and day out, week after week, year after year he's walked this domain, hunting for sustenance the way his ancestors have for countless generations. Before much of this land was locked up in parks, refuges, forests and wilderness lines drawn by the federal government; before the U.S bought the land from Russia; before the Russians made first landfall in 1741.

I saw him earlier while walking on the footpath. It was only a short glimpse of dark fur moving through the trees, but it was sufficient to know he embodied the very essence my search.

A combination of respect and fear filled my mind as I left the safety of the developed trail to pursue him into the thick vegetation of the Chugach National Forest. This afternoon I am the hunter and he is the prey.

Light and shadows mix as the sun dances with the clouds in the sky above. The whole light show is filtered by an old growth spruce canopy above, giving the perfect conditions of camouflage for the coloring of his dark coat. These are the kind of trees that make the perfect timber to build rustic log cabins and lodges with "Great Rooms" to match the openness of this land. My "Realtree" fleece jacket and matching pants are only a cheap ploy compared to his natural coat.

Sound has been the thread that has tied us together for the past 20 minutes. As he moves to escape my chase, I hear him and make my next move. He hears me and counters again. It is a game of chess, each player trying to out-maneuver the other, second-guessing our opponent's next move. For years he has been the pursuer; now he is pursued. Another twig breaks with a snap under my boot. I stop. Leaves rustle to my right as he tries to move away.

Let no one tell you that these are "dumb" animals that deserve your pity. These are powerful, ingenious creatures that live and die by their wits and cunning. They deserve our utmost admiration.

The minutes tick by slowly during the match. I hear him make another move and decide to change my strategy. No longer being quiet, I walk straight toward him. As I near his position, I freeze. I'm trying to force his hand. I'm uncomfortably close and not moving. I don't think he knows my exact position, at least that's what I'm banking on. I'm hoping these factors will drive him into a panic. My presence this close should coerce him into making a fatal decision. Like a troll hit by sunlight, I stand.

I feel the ever-present breeze off Turnagain Arm as it brushes my face. All is silent except the rhythmic pulsing of my accelerated heartbeat as the adrenaline-charged blood courses through my veins – thump, thump....thump, thump..... thump, thump. Then...a movement...the sure-fire betrayal of any quarry. A hairy untamed silhouette slowly begins to materialize; it starts with the glint of an eye, followed by the shape of a head, ears, and four legs with sharp claws. The anatomy for a one shot kill is in full view as I ever so slowly lift my rifle to my shoulder. If he were much bigger I'd go for the two shot method. One shot to the front shoulder first to knock him down, the second to the vitals. He's no Boone and Crockett record setter, but he's no runt either.

As I place the sights, a panic runs through my mind. What if I miss? What if the first shot only grazes the clawed beast? Will I be charged? Can I get off another shot from my rifle or should I reach for my sidearm? Why didn't I bring someone along for a back-up shot? Can I back out now?... NO!...I fight back these feelings of vulnerability, and whisper to myself, "It's as good a day to die as any other."

I settle the gun into my shoulder again, I count the front sight: one. The rear sight: two. The animal's vital area: three. I return my focus to the front sight, squeeze the trigger and with a loud "BANG" the copper covered slug finds it's mark. The beast falls over and collapses on the woodland floor.

My approach is cautious as I near the furry lump from the rear, a trick used by the Inupiat of

Alaska's North Slope when they check polar bears they have shot. There's nothing more frightening than having an animal merely stunned, springing back to life when you're only feet or inches away. While that has never happened to me personally, I don't want to experience that kind of wilderness deceit today.

Only two feet, just twenty-four inches in front of my feet lies this denizen of the forest. I didn't see it breathing, but still I could not be sure. I took my eyes off it for just a second and locate a long alder branch on the ground. I grab it with my left hand and poke the carcass. Not even the hint of life is left in the body. A sigh of relief ripples through me. The battle of wits has reached fruition as I mutter, "Checkmate, my friend."

I yell to my boys Jake and Cale, 7 and 5 years old, respectively. They are not far behind me on the trail. They come running up and yell excitedly "Daddy! You got another one!" and "Can I have this one's tail?" I try to remain humble in front of them but, yeah, I actually just bagged my third of the day and in only about an hour and a half. Better yet, just 40 miles south of Anchorage.

My trusty rifle was my Marlin Model 60 semi-automatic .22. The quarry was the Great Alaskan

Red Squirrel of which the Alaska Department of Fish and Game offers "no bag limit". Sure, they don't pack as much meat as some of their cousins like the Alaskan ground squirrel or gray squirrels I've hunted in the Lower 48, but we can make our dinners out of these three nonetheless. OK I'll throw in a little rice, too.

I just had a successful world class hunt at relatively no cost, save a bit of fuel and a few .22 shells. Not only that, but my children just participated in the time honored tradition of "hunting with Dad". It's a tradition I learned from my father and he from his and so on through all the generations before us. I think my first kill, not counting neighborhood birds, might have been a squirrel. I was excited for the squirrel hunt and I know my kids were too! They ask to go often (even unprompted sometimes).

Now, before you start to question my machismo, let me say that I've been charged by a grizzly and a moose or two, kicked by a white-tail deer, been face to face with an angry cougar, chased by a rattlesnake and, at one time or another, hunted just about every critter on this continent. And yes, seeing a rodent still moves me.

I contend that with the right frame of mind and the right caliber, whether you're hunting cape buffalo in Zimbabwe with a .458 Winchester mag or hunting a common house mouse over bait on your back porch with a Red Rider Daisy B.B. Gun (don't laugh, I actually do it, a fact my neighbors often talk about when they are questioning my sanity), any hunt is still a kick in the pants and a tradition worth passing on to your kids. For it is the practice and pursuit itself that makes the hunt, not the type of prey you are pursuing. Sure, it is a squirrel – but a hunt is a hunt, just like a Harley is a Harley, and a dollar a dollar.

Author's sons posing with the morning's bounty

Caribou seem to be the most trusting. Thank God

Trust Your Scope

Hunting in general is filled with trust issues. I trust that my ATV would run. I trust that its tires wouldn't go flat. I trust that I wouldn't get lost, even though I'd never been on that trail before. I trust that Remington made every shell I will load in my gun perfectly. I trust the weather. Why, then, can't I trust a scope? Thank God I could trust that the caribou would stick around through all that shooting.

You can probably identify with the excitement building within me as the August 10 opening for caribou passed Sunday morning. I knew it was only a matter of picking my day and I would take my first "big game" of the season. I brought an old Remington Mohawk, model 600 6mm along for this express purpose. It was my fathers' rifle, a feather-light little gun that I used as a youth to hunt deer back in Montana. He sent it to me the winter before. When I unpacked it, I noticed one big change. It had a scope.

Normally a scope wouldn't be such a big deal, but for me, being a traditionalist (OK, too stubborn to change), it was more of a betrayal. How could my dad, the man who preached the greatness of the sharpshooters of iron sights, put a scope on this icon of my youth? Was he playing a cruel joke on me? Didn't he trust my steely-eyed marksmanship? Maybe he had whimped out in his old age! Or maybe one day he had an extra 100 bucks and finally just put a scope on the damn thing. Whatever the reason I figured it's time I embrace the 20th century (yeah, with only three years left in it) and learn to shoot with a scope.

It's not that I don't have scopes on most of my rifles, 'cause I do. Nor am I pretending I don't take most of my larger game with a scope, 'cause I do. Nonetheless most of my shooting was always with iron sights. The move to scopes was actually a slow transition that began about seven years ago. Now the last vestige of my firearm collection to not be crowned with a scope is my .22. It also happens to be the rifle I use the most.

I just don't have trust in scopes. So when I got this one I looked for help. I took the 6mm to my friends at the local shooting range for a boresighting, then I went to field test it. It was dead on at 100 yds. I was ready. I had shot a good 40 rounds and felt confident that those little cross hairs told the tale of where the 100 grains of copper-covered lead would end up. At least for now!

On August 14th work ended at 5:30 p.m. In the back of my truck sat a Polaris six-wheeler. I like these ATVs because they never get stuck (well almost never,) they have power to spare, they have a cargo bed like a pick-up and I guess mainly because it belonged to the company and I didn't have to buy or rent it. I drove to a friend's house where a trail began in his back yard, and started across the tundra at about 7 p.m. The trail was a bit bumpy so the going was slow.

About two miles out I was glassing a slope when I saw a small bull grazing on some lichen half a mile away. I continued on the trail for another ten minutes and stopped to glass again. When I looked where the bull had been, he was gone. Then suddenly I saw him again, closer this time, walking toward the trail I was on. I drove my ATV ... sorry, I mean I drove the company ATV ... a few hundred yards and got in range. I hopped off the machine, took out the rifle and leaned it across the front rack of the vehicle. I remember thinking how light the rifle felt compared to my 30.06 or the .338 Magnum I usually pack.

He wasn't a large bull, probably a two-year old. He was facing directly at me standing still on a gently-sloping hill covered with tundra and small thickets of alder. I figured him to be about 200 yards so I held the cross hairs four inches above his head when I squeezed the trigger. The report rang and I waited for the ungulate to fall with a thud to the multi-color splashed tundra. As I looked through the four power scope, he just shook his head just like those African water buffalo on the Discovery Channel when they're at the watering hole and flies are bugging them.

Whitetails or muleys, back home, would sometimes stand for 30 seconds or a minute or two before lying down to die when hit by the 100 grain slug fired from the quick little Mohawk. The 6mm is so fast and tiny that sometimes I don't even think they realized they had been hit. I thought this might be the case with the caribou as well. He shook his head a couple more times and began grazing again. My optimism fell along with my self esteem.

How could I be so foolish to think a scope would still be accurate? After all, it had been months since I last sighted it in. Silently I cursed myself for not taking the time to sight it in again, right before the hunt. Why did I have to be so cheap? Was ammo for this pea-shooter really THAT expensive? The old man must be playing a practical joke on me knowing full well that scopes go out, way out, real quickly and real easy. The slightest bump could throw it totally out of whack! At least I was sure of it!

The bull was grazing broadside to me and obviously didn't feel much threat. Would you? I decided that it must be shooting low so I raised a good 12 inches above his head and squeezed the trigger. I could hear the soft thud as the bullet struck the damp tundra. The tundra is more like layer upon layer of damp moss than it is like ground. There is no tell-tale dust to let you know where your lead hits.

The shirttail relative of Rudolph raised his head to look at me, paused then began grazing again. "It must be shooting to the left then," I rationalized. I corrected for this glaring error and squeezed the trigger. Boom! The caribou took off running like Ben Johnson trying to avoid a urinalysis. Finally a hit! Nothing left to do now except wait for him to stop, drop, and do a flop.

After about 50 yards he slowed to a walk. I waited. He must be ready to fall. He began grazing again. I looked in disbelief. I was sure my father was hiding behind a ridge, laughing maniacally at me behind his binoculars. If I could only find dad, I'd give him a piece of my mind.... and his scope.

I jumped on the 6-wheeler again and drove straight toward him. At 80 yards I could see him in detail with the naked eye. He looked directly at me and began walking the same direction. He stopped as I dismounted the green Polaris. He watched with curiosity as I leveled the rifle at him. Surely at 75 yards the defective scope must be shooting high. I aimed at his brisket and shot. He ran like the wind...50 yards... quartering to my left... stopped

...looked at me momentarily... and began grazing again!

Wearily, I climbed back on my tundra transport and tried to get closer. As I approached, he withdrew. Finally, I stopped and began a slow cumbersome crawl down the three feet off the seat to the ground. I lifted the bulky weight of the weapon to my shoulder and rested its massive girth on the front of the All Terrain Vehicle. A couple more missed shots were fired, each report getting the same dull thud answer as the lead belted the lichen.

I had four shells remaining so I gave up trying to second guess where the faulty scope is set. I set the cross hairs just behind his lower front quarter. It's where I would normally place the bead, if I only had my trusty old-faithful iron sites. I let out a big breath and squeeze. The muzzle blast was followed by the muffled "whack" of a flesh-covered bone being shattered by a piece of metal.

At 100 yards the bullet hit about two inches to the left of where the cross hairs were placed! The bull leapt forward and landed on three hooves. His left front leg rotated like a ZZ Top guitar. He knelt and rested.

I gave him a few minutes to stiffen up as I put my rifle back into its soft-case and gathered my composure. I drove within 20 yards of the animal, pulled my 9 mm pistol from my backpack and dispatched the regal beast.

As I said a prayer of thanks, I noticed a small hole at the base of his right antler. It was... oh.. I don't know... about 6 mm in diameter? OK, it was exactly 6 mm. My first shot had hit his antler, that's why he was shaking his head. It must have felt like Quazimoto was ringing the bells at the Notre Dame inside his head. Two inches lower would have been an instant caribou rag doll! There was also a small hole through his lower right rear leg, the hit that sent him running

like Ben Johnson. Also I noticed an eight inch gash (all right, I'm a guy. It was probably six inches) as if someone had grazed his brisket with a knife, the third hit. The fourth hit had struck the vitals apparently because that's where I had aimed.

I loaded the "bou" on to the rig and drove out. Except for getting stuck in one bog, the trip back to my friend's house was pretty uneventful. I was home and had him hanging in my garage by 10:30 p.m. Now that I recall the story I still find it unbelievable that the scope fixed itself for that last shot. I must have been real lucky and bumped it back into the correct position.

NAKNEK

It's still 70 miles to the ocean, but it is connected

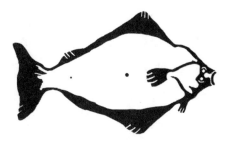

River Halibut

There are a great many stories told over the years that aren't limited by the truth. Some of these stories grow as they're handed down through the ages. You can't really call them lies; they're more like "local myths." Local myths are OK, 'cause everyone knows they are just for fun, kind of like the World Wrestling Federation. However, Alaska is a land where the more outrageous a story is, the more likely it is to be true. This is one of those hard to believe but true Alaska stories. It could also be the beginning of a local myth if everyone who knew better played along ... just for fun.

We arrived at Kevin's house about 3 p.m., pulling the 26-foot boat. We were coming in from a productive half-day of halibut fishing in Cook Inlet. Kevin Zimmerman lived in Ninilchik, an old Russian village on the coast of the Kenai Peninsula, some 180 road miles south of Anchorage. He ran a fishing guide service called "The Butt-Chasers". There are a plethora of local colloquialisms regarding "fishing for butts," catching 'em, and the like.

We had been out "fishing for butts" throughout the late morning tide and had both caught our limit. Kevin let me take his daily limit of two halibut home. I flopped the four flat fish into a few plastic bags. Kevin asked if I was going to fillet them. I said I'd do it at home because with the four-hour drive ahead of me I wanted to get started in that general direction.

I drove for about an hour and a half, past Kasilof, through Soldotna, past Sterling and into the mountains, but something just wasn't right. I couldn't figure out what it was, but the gnawing in my guts continued to grow. When I saw the aqua-marine color, I finally discovered the root of the gut-twisting turmoil inside me - the Kenai River!!! But I had seen the river before, so what was so different and so alluring this time? Suddenly, it dawned on me! It was the first week of August, the reds (sockeye salmon) were in thick in early August! The Kenai had been calling me! I took the next turn out near the water.

As I took out my rod, the giddiness was almost overwhelming 'cause I knew what was about to happen. All thoughts of getting home by 8 p.m. were instantly erased from my memory. It was sunny, the river was a brilliant aquamarine and there were 900,000 sockeye salmon moving along its shores.

I tied a "coho" fly on the end of my line with an improved clinch knot and stuck a couple big split-shot about three feet above it. On the third roll cast, I set the hook on a nice eight pounder! We fought for awhile, then up to the shore and my waiting hand-carved Fish-Bonker. Smack! The red's eyes did the "quiver of death" as I dispatched the silver slab of delectable fish flesh with one blow from the "Bonker". A couple more deft casts and my line went taut again as another red pulled against the drag of my reel. A few minutes later, another sockeye dun gone!

I decided to catch and release for a while since the next one I keep would fill my daily limit of three. As I was releasing one of a dozen or more I let go, a motor home pulled up and out stepped four men. When I walked to the top of the bank I glanced over and saw "Texas" on the license plate.

I caught a couple more fish, including a nice Dolly Varden and a little rainbow, but decided it was probably time to fillet my salmon and move along.

The Texans were full of questions about reds as I carved the deep red flesh from the bones of the salmon, " What kind of fly do you use? How much weight?   What color?" I showed them the set up I was using and told them about the "roll cast" used to present the fly in the proper manner to hook these particular plankton feeders.

The Texans were busy beating the water to a froth as I finished with the last salmon and decided, since I was cutting already, to take out the halibut for filleting as well. It didn't take long for the white meat of the halibut to grab their attention.

I was cutting up the second one when the first Texan asked, "What kind of fish is that?" I told them it was a halibut and the next question was so ludicrous to me that I found it hard to answer. He asked "Did you catch THEM here too?"

"No," I told them. Then I heard another voice take over. It sounded just like my voice but it was like an out-of-body experience listening to this new voice, using my mouth, while it said, "I caught them downstream a-ways."

"How far?" they asked. I looked them right square-in-the-eyes when the voice said, "a couple hundred yards."

The story was now presented. I tried to look nonchalant as I continued to fillet. One of them piped up and said "But I thought halibut were saltwater fish?"

"They are" said the voice "But this time of year they follow the salmon upstream to feed on their dying carcasses." The words came right out of my mouth before I knew who said them.

"Wow," said the Texans.

"As a matter of fact" the voice continued, "Only the really big ones can swim up past this point in the river cause the current gets too strong for anything under 100 lbs."

I was in awe of the story myself. It almost sounded plausible. The voice told these visitors to get a three to five ounce lead weight and place it a couple feet up from the streamer fly, that I so graciously gave each of them, and cast the weight way out into the middle of the current.

"When you feel it stop, cross his eyes! Set the hook hard! If it's a big river halibut, he'll just hold in place. You gotta keep the pressure on him. It's the only way he'll get tired out." The voice also told them it would probably feel like a "Lower 48" snag, but to keep the pressure on

cause he could sit like a stump for 20 minutes or even longer. "But when he gets ready to take off ....Look out, Jack!!! Most locals," the voice continued, "never actually land river halibut, they just hook them for the pleasure of fighting them until the line breaks."

The Texans were entranced as the voice spun its yarn. They asked for directions to "where the big ones lie." The voice began again and my hand, of its own accord, raised and pointed out a trail which led down to a bend in the river some half a mile upstream.

Like children heading out to go play in the park, they skipped down the path until all was silent. I thought about following to take pictures but decided not to. When you really connect swinging a baseball bat, you don't need to see it clear the fence to know it's a home run.

I drove home, grinning all the way, wondering what "story" they would tell their friends back home in Texas, about the big river halibut in the Kenai who broke all their lines. But I'm sure they were all incredible fights. Hell, one probably even broke water! You know, I hear only the biggest of big Kenai River halibut will do that.*

*Author's note: To the Texas fishermen out there who fell for my trick, please forgive me. Please, also, don't hunt me down and shoot me. But, if you insist on seeking me out for some kind of sick revenge, remember that Alaska is two-and-a-half times as big as Texas. Good luck tracking me down.

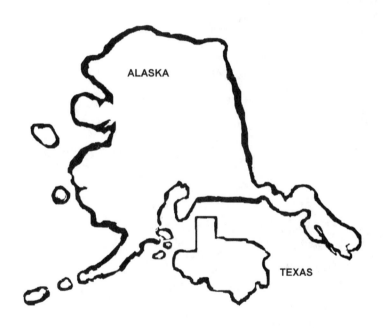

Any given gravel road, any given snowless morning

Grouse Netting

Hunters get stuck in ruts. What I mean is that there are a lot of tried and true methods we all use, most of the time without question. Tree stands for various types of game, drives through thickets to flush white-tails, dogs for pheasant, and decoys for waterfowl. We use these methods mainly because they work. It's also usually the way someone taught us.

But every now and then an innovator comes on the scene and shows us a new way to do things. Sometimes the new method is really an old, forgotten method, re-invented with modern technology. Such is the case with grouse netting.

Spruce grouse are an abundant upland game bird in much of Alaska. Drive any gravel road on any snowless morning and you will probably see a few "spruce chickens" standing alongside, picking at small pebbles, trying to fill the leathery pouch in their digestive tract. The rock-filled gizzard helps the fowl by grinding up food, a useful substitute for teeth.

The grouse relies on camouflage to evade predators. The gray and white coloring actually does blend in with the gravel road. If a predator comes too close, the spruce chicken takes a quick, but short, flight into a nearby spruce tree, where its coloring and its ability to stand stock still makes it all but invisible. In general it's an effective strategy against animal predators, and spruce chickens are always plentiful in Alaska.

Unfortunately for the little, round, football-shaped fowl, its silhouette is a dead giveaway to the human eye. Usually, stopping your vehicle twenty yards away, stepping outside and letting a head-splitting round fly from your .22, or a smattering of pellets from a .410 is the preferred method for harvest of this tasty, large-breasted table fare. Even if the bird evades the first shot, or second, or even the third, its short flight rarely takes it out of reach of your rifle sights. Its life-long strategy is camouflage, not speedy escape.

Enter our innovator. I will call him "Bob White" to protect the guilty, because the grouse hunting method you're about to learn is not quite permissible under the Alaska Department of Fish and Game regulations; at least, not yet. To Bob and his cohorts, it's not even hunting. It's a full-blown competitive sporting event, at least the equal of NFL Sundays, and certainly more important than the NBA All-Star game.

Most gravel roads in grouse-infested areas are traveled often enough to train the fledgling to take flight early enough to avoid being turned into a street pizza. However, on some roads in Alaska this evolutionary education hasn't yet occurred. The birds often wait, relying on their protective coloration, hoping the speeding chunk of steel will take an alternate path, completely missing the miniature Thanksgiving dinner waiting by the roadside. Sadly for the grouse, that tactic leaves a lot of Alaskan scavengers with full stomachs.

Our Bob White is a seasoned man of construction, having spent all his life as a resident of the Great Land. He is also a seasoned outdoorsman, excelling in hunting, fishing and trapping. These are a way of life for our Bob. His consumption of beef and other domestic fare is confined to those occasions when he is forced to dine in restaurants. His preference, usually loudly and proudly verbalized, is wild game. I have seen him pass a carefully prepared meal of New York steak and linguine with clam sauce for a caribou tongue sandwich.

During one field season, Bob was mobilizing for the start of a new project, or "mobbing" as it's referred to in construction circles. The project was to re-surface a remote gravel road in "Bush" Alaska. About a week into the process, Bob requisitioned the company to send him a small hand net. Not knowing what it was for, indeed not caring what it was for, the expediter, who will also have to remain anonymous for the same reason as Bob (avoiding jail), found him a trout net. Bob was almost giddy with joy when it was handed to him.

Bob took the net and the young expediter and traveled via floatplane to the project. After work was complete for the day, Bob and his apprentice went for a drive along the road on ATV's. This particular road sees fewer vehicles than most, even for Alaska. Therefore, the grouse are far less skittish than elsewhere.

Bob drove the road at about thirty miles per hour. Suddenly, he'd seem to tense up, like a retriever spotting a pheasant in a stubble field. His driving became more focused and directed. The silhouette he was aiming toward tensed too.

The speed remained steady, his net-carrying left hand cocked like a tennis player about to return a volley with a backhand smash. The grouse began to fidget, nervously. Then at about ten feet, the grouse abandoned all hope of concealment. Up it sprang, wings fluttering in an attempt to turn the leap into an actual flight of escape. But before wings could catch up with the kinetic energy of the jump, the net came forward, surrounding the bird and with a quick turn of the wrist, in a cloud of feathers, the small net closed any avenue of escape.

Bob then abruptly stopped the four-wheeler, reached in the net and with the same wrist motion you would use to turn one of those cheap little party noise makers, the grouse was quickly dispatched.

Quickly breasting the bird, he placed the featherless meat into the cooler, which was strapped on the rear of the ATV. Then he looked up and told his awed apprentice, "That was the 'left-handed cross catch."

Grouse netting had become quite a competitive sport between Bob and his friends a year or two earlier. However, grouse netting is a dangerous sport, not like the other sissy sports, such as football or hockey. To the uninitiated, grouse netting often appears simple and safe, but such is not the case. A champion grouse netter needs great concentration on the target to complete his netting. Unfortunately, that means they must take their eyes off the road as they endeavor to capture the little sucker. The occasional head-on collision with a large spruce tree is considered a minor impediment to a competitive grouse netter.

And, of course, traveling remote roads in Alaska, especially on ATV's, one must take into account big brown furry things like caribou, moose and grizzly bears who take offense when tiny little humans and their toys go buzzing through their stomping grounds. Grouse netters have learned first hand the origin of the term stomping grounds.

Bob explained that, at first, with the throttle of most ATV's being right handed, they tried the two-man method of grouse netting. This seemed the answer to the not-coordinated left hand often missing the bird. In the two-man method, one drove and the other sat precariously on the front rack with eyes forward and net in hand. The driver would then be notified of a looming target at the side of the road and drive directly toward the prey. Upon arrival the front man, or "netter," would have an easy reach and capture.

This seemed like the answer until, traveling at thirty miles per hour, Bob and his "netter" turned a corner to see, at close range, a beautiful example of a large Alaskan brown bear standing in the middle of the road directly in front of them.

At first, it seemed simple to Bob. Just hit the brakes and stop. Easy enough! Consequently, he locked 'em up. Not bad in theory. But there were consequences he hadn't thought about in making his spur-of-the-moment decision, such as Newton's First Law of Motion (which states, "every object in a state of uniform motion tends to remain in that state of motion unless an external force is applied to it," in this case the brakes of the ATV).

First, it takes a good distance to stop an ATV at thirty miles per hour on a gravel road, and he didn't have a whole lot of room between him and the bear. Second, the netter can't anticipate the braking and ends up rolling off the luggage rack, directly into the path of the bear.

For the novice, be advised that rolling on gravel, or a couple of rolls as the case may be, can drive small sharp rocks into the meaty part of your elbows, knees and other assorted body parts, which is another impediment for the competitive grouse-netter to consider. Not to be ignored, rolling and bouncing along the road to stop at the feet of an extremely puzzled bruin, also presents special challenges. Experienced

grouse netters can testify that a small hand net offers inadequate protection against a grizzly.

Surviving that experience, the determined grouse netters tried placing the netter on the back, but smacking the net against the driver's face during attempted capture discouraged the use of that particular formation early in the game.

In the end the one man, left-handed operation was the answer. Needless to say, left-handed competitors stayed atop the standings in the early part of the season, until right-handed competitors learned to adapt with their left hand, much as right-handed baseball players learn to catch a baseball with their left hand.

During this particular day of grouse netting, Bob and his young student saw three fly back out of the net, but successfully caught twelve. They also had to send one ATV back to Anchorage for repairs, having discovered that throwing gears into reverse at thirty miles per hour takes a heavy toll on machinery. Still, it seemed preferable to running headlong into an astonished bear standing in the middle of a gravel road. *

* Author's Note: To any enforcement officer of any agency with jurisdiction over issues concerning fish and game, the taking of, the harassing of, the viewing of or any other activity with or near fish and or game. If you find some of these stories contrary to laws that you have the option, responsibility, or requirement to enforce, then that part was all made up.

Grouse Netting   Painting by Mike Ortega

"I think we're going to need a bigger boat"

Shark

Fishing in Alaska holds a certain charm and mystique all to itself. If you ask most avid anglers about Alaskan fishing, you'd probably hear "kings." Kings, or "chinook" (*Oncorhynchus tshawytscha*), are the most sought after game fish in our state. But why? Pound for pound kings aren't the strongest fighters. Most anglers agree they're not even the best tasting salmon. So why do we spend countless man-hours chasing this fish? EGO! That's right, Ego. The king, because of its enormous size (and name), has always been the 'king' of ego fish, until now.

Resurrection Bay was jam-packed with silvers one August morning as television sports director John Carpenter and I arrived at the

Seward boat harbor. Twelve pound salmon were actually landing on the dock as they leapt out of the water trying to shake sea-lice from their scales.

We met a longtime friend, Captain Bob Candopolis, at his boat, the "Legend". Bob is a partner in The Saltwater Safari Company, with assets counting two fifty-foot charter boats, top of the line A-1 gear, a lifetime of fishing experience and some pretty good showmanship to round it out.

Along with Captain Bob was Captain Kent Mongreig and deck hands Steve and Mark. Bob picked "The Legend" for our shark hunt. She's a fifty-foot Delta with twin 435 horse diesel engines that make a cruising speed of 28 knots just another day on the water.

The coast of Montague Island in Prince William Sound was to be our hunting grounds, but the seas were a bit too rough to leave the protection of Resurrection Bay. Even in August the winds create waves that start small near the coast of British Columbia, intensify through the Gulf, and can smash small planets by the time they hit the coast of Alaska. That morning our search was confined to the bay.

We departed the boat harbor at 8 am. Bob told us to keep our eyes peeled for splashing near the shore. This would be our sign of sharks. At 8:20 a.m. we saw what we had come for. It was the great salmon shark (*Lamna ditropis)* and he was on the prowl just south of Thumb Cove some seven miles from Seward.

The salmon shark is in the same family as the great white, the mako, and its Atlantic counterpart, the porbeagle, otherwise known as the mackerel shark. It's a man-eater. Fortunately, in Alaska, there aren't a lot of swimmers hanging around wading at the beach. Salmon sharks grow to between six and a half and eight and a half feet long and weighing several hundred pounds. Unconfirmed reports exist of salmon shark reaching as much as 14 feet long, however the largest confirmed reports indicate a maximum total length of approximately 10 feet.

This time of year the sharks follow huge schools of silver salmon as they head for spawning streams. They chase salmon up into the shallows and take them on the surface. As I understand it, for every shark you see, there are 20 or more below.

Captain Bob grabbed the five and a half foot Penn "Tuna Stick" outfitted with a Penn International reel. On the end of the hundred pound test mono line was a fifteen-foot steel leader made from 3/16 inch airplane cable.

The boat was doing a slow troll over the area. He let the bait, a large herring with a rubber squid, drop behind the boat on a free-spool, the weight of the leader being enough to cause the set-up to sink. After about 90 feet had peeled off Captain Bob set the fighting drag to half, and with the boat still moving, slowly reeled the bait toward the boat. This caused the herring to spin rapidly.

On the second retrieve, as the reel began to give up line at an alarming rate, Bob stopped and turned to Captain Kent at the helm and yelled "He's taking it, he's taking it. Get ready."

When these beasts first take the herring or any other animal, they just take it in lightly in their teeth. They shake their head from side to side as they swim away letting their teeth tear the flesh, then they move up another bite.

Bob let her run out about 60 yards, then figuring he could finally get a good hook-set he moved the fighting drag to "full" and told Kent to "Hit it!"

Both engines roared as they were gunned wide open. Simultaneously Bob pulled back on the rod like young Arthur trying to pull the sword from the stone. The combination of these actions drove the razor sharp barb deep into the fish's jaws.

Fishing for these monsters is thrilling and so far you've only heard what it's like to set the hook.

When it was my turn the first thing the crew did was outfit me with the necessary armor for battle. A stand-up fighting belt was put around my waist and a thick leather harness was put over my shoulders and buckled to the Penn International.

As the fight began, this aquatic locomotive was running directly away from the boat. I could do nothing to stop her. I watched as it appeared the fish was about to spool my reel. Captain Kent saw the problem immediately and maneuvered the boat accordingly.

Big sharks are smart. Sensing the reduced pull against her massive jaws, she turned and ran directly at the boat. My right arm burned as I reeled in the slack.

The crew of the *Legend* had tangled with more than one wily carnivore and reacted quickly in helping me get this one under control. A good crew and experienced captain are as vital as a sharp hook in these parts.

Now that we were both settled into fighting position, I began to understand just what my opponent was made of. Cartilage and flesh with a decidedly predatory disposition. This was an animal that did nothing but swim, kill, and eat 24 hours a day.

I began to pump the rod, gaining a couple of feet with each pull. I had a lot of ground to make up. As I brought this eating machine about forty feet from the boat, I began to feel its head shake. I knew I was in for another back-breaking run. Again the Penn International sang as it gave up line to this underwater Scud missile.

Every inch I had gained back and more was lost. At 40 minutes into the fight my legs were feeling like noodles left too long in boiling water (at that moment, if you would have thrown me against the wall I'm sure I would have stuck).

Unlike Marlin fishing, people in Alaska don't use fighting chairs. We stand toe to toe with our big game fish. We sound kind of stupid don't we? Captain Bob slid a cooler behind me to use as a seat. As I sat down the fish had moved under the boat. Captain Kent moved the boat forward to plane the fish, giving me better control.

Once again I began the arduous task of gaining line. My arms and back were burning, but I still had some distance to go before they were toast. The stand-up fighting belt I was using, however, was pressing unduly against my stomach muscles. Funny how a belt called a "stand-up" model doesn't quite fit the same when you're sitting down. Finally my abs were spent.

As the shark began its third long run, I can't even remember how many short runs she made, I called to my partner, John Carpenter. At 48 minutes into the fight the crew transferred the belt, harness, and rod to him. I had to go lie down for a while to regain my composure. O.K. so I was a little nauseous too.

When I returned, John was watching the line disappear in the first of three long runs the shark would take on him.

As this great predator of the sea did to me it did to Carp as well. After 25 minutes of battle, John wanted no more of the fight. Luckily for us the shark was done too.

As John brought the beast to the boat one last time, Captain Bob and the crew quickly dispatched her. It still cracks me up to see a fully grown Greek man running around the stern of a boat shooting a .40 caliber Beretta at a fish. (He actually shot one in mid-air in the head as it jumped. It's on video.)

We were all humbled by this creature of the sea. We hurt for days after, but our egos were fully re-charged. The icing on this 575-pound cake? It's also a great tasting fish.

Looking at US as food

Black Bear

When I first decided to go, I wasn't even going to take a gun. And then when I did, I only grabbed my .44 pistol. I just thought my two boys and I were going to catch some salmon. I hadn't expected a bear. I really didn't even plan to be there that week.

I was just wrapping up my final day at work in Anchorage before a week of vacation when Suzy, the cute little blonde receptionist, paged me. On the phone was Craig Ketchum, owner of Ketchum Air, the largest air taxi service on Lake Hood, which just happened to be the largest sea-plane base in the world. I was the spokesman for Ketchum's radio and television ads, and had been for years. Craig was calling to see what I was doing in my seven whole days off. I told him I planned to fish for kings on the Kenai late in the week, but I was taking my two boys camping wherever we could find fish.

Ketchum not only had the baddest fleet of planes on the lake, they also had remote cabins and houseboats all over Alaska right in the middle of some of the best fishing and hunting the state offers.

Craig told me he had the big cabin at Alexander Creek available and, if I got the kids together and down to the dock by 6 p.m., he'd fly us over. Now I like living the "Life of Riley" as well as the next guy, so I agreed. That gave me about seven hours to get everything together and, like the true procrastinator that I am, I went home and took a nap. Needless to say, by 5 p.m. I was in a frenzied mess trying to wrap up loose ends and get every thing packed for the 6 p.m. departure.

As I was packing ... wait, who am I trying to kid? As I was throwing everything I could see into a drybag in a last ditch effort to appear to be organized, I looked at my old Ruger Super Blackhawk .44 magnum, my bear repellent. My first instinct was to throw it and a box of shells in the bag, too. But I started thinking; Alexander Creek, like anyplace that has a lot of fish within a fifty-mile radius of Anchorage, is a pretty popular destination, meaning lots of people. I've been there dozens of times and never seen a bear. I almost put the gun back down but then at the last minute I threw it in the bag "just because". I've learned never to go anywhere outside the city without some form of gun powder-propelled protection.

The flight was pretty damn cool. I just never seem to lose the giddiness I feel every time the floatplane I'm riding in lifts off the water. I can't imagine how it must feel when you're four and seven years old as my boys were. We landed, unloaded and waved good-bye to Charlie, our pilot, watching him disappear as he headed back to base.

That night was relaxed and quiet. I use the term "night" loosely because July in Alaska doesn't really get dark - at about 2 a.m. in town you could still drive without your headlights. Still, we had a nice dinner, drowned each other in bug dope, went for a late walk and retired to bed. The boys were asleep before their heads hit the pillows.

Is it my imagination, or do children recharge faster than adults? The morning started with the boys bouncing up and down on my stomach, a game that was cute when they were 1 and 3 but that was 30 pounds ago. Each! Displaying remarkable courage, I got up. The sky was clear and Mount Susitna, or as the locals call it, "Sleeping Lady", rose up, towering behind us. We ate breakfast and went fishing in the twelve-foot aluminum boat with the three-horse outboard supplied by Ketchum.

About 7 p.m. the last of the day-fishermen got on the last floatplanes and flew back to town. We were hanging out in our cabin talkin' guy stuff when Cale, my youngest, decided we should go fishing, now that everybody else had left. We dragged the boat down to the water and put on an engine. These three-horse outboards are notorious for being difficult. I'm usually lucky enough to figure out the problems with them quickly but 30 feet from shore this one decided to die on us. The creek was about 50 yards across, a foot and a half deep and had little to no current so close to the Susitna river.

As I was pulling to start the motor, I noticed a good-sized black bear back on the shore. He was right where we had just dragged our boat into the water. I said, "Hey boys look at the bear." While my kids were looking at the bear I got out the camera and took a couple snapshots. As I took the second picture, the bear took a couple steps toward us. Normally this wouldn't be such a big deal but when this started he was only 40 feet or so away, now he had closed the gap to just 30 feet.

Bears in Alaska sometimes become habituated to humans. Some of these bears associate humans with food, and occasionally bears learn that if they get close to humans the humans will often move a good distance away and leave dead, fresh fish right there for the bears to eat. I believe this was one such bear.

I left my gun up in the cabin, so as the bear was approaching us I grabbed the florescent green oar in the boat, lifted it up in the air like a baseball bat and began to tell the bear in what my kids call "Daddy's serious voice" that, if he walked out to this boat, I was going "to kick his ass." The kids were looking at me pretty funny like, 'What's wrong with Dad?' The bear took another step closer, I raised the oar and my voice a bit higher as I repeated my threat of physical violence.

The bruin seemed to be more agitated at this point. He walked back to shore and headed for our cabin. That situation wasn't sitting well with me either. He pawed at the door. I tried to convince myself that he didn't know about the bacon in the cooler. I yelled a bit more. He slowly ambled down the trail to the next cabin and started pawing at its door.

I rowed the boat to shore, keeping "Boo Boo" in sight, hustled the boys into our cabin and grabbed my pistol. My oldest asked me if I was going to kill the bear. I told him I was going to try and that they were both to stay in the cabin, "no mater what you hear. " It was 10:30 p.m. and I knew if anything happened the pilots would be by for coffee by 6 a.m., so I closed the door and started down the trail.

The bear was on the porch of the cabin next to ours scratching and pushing on the door. He looked to be about a five and a half or six-footer. I was at the cabin earlier so I knew it was empty. As I got within 60 yards he started acting a bit different. He seemed to be nervous. He turned from the door and backhanded the metal garbage can, sending the lid sailing into the trees. I sensed he knew I was there. He looked like he was about to run, whatever that means, only I wasn't sure if he was going to run away from me or toward me. I drew a bead on his front shoulder and squeezed the trigger. He shuttered for an instant, then tore off the porch toward some near-by bushes.

Often when I've shot deer they've run through the trees 30 or 40 feet before falling dead in their tracks; I expected the same from the bear. As I approached the bushes, you guessed it, no bear. I ran 20 yards further down the trail and stood at the edge of a draw.

Time almost stood still. So many thoughts raced through my mind. Where did he go? Why can't I find any spoor? Is this my destiny, to wound a great and powerful bear so it can maul some unsuspecting tent camper to death? Do people do jail time for that? How do I get my ex-wife in that tent?

Suddenly, I heard a twig snap up the draw to my right. I picked my way tree by tree. I traveled 75 yards. Suddenly I spied movement! There, only 40 yards away, a brown snout surrounded by a black face. The bear was looking my direction, slowly rocking back and forth.

I took another step to get a better position, drew a bead right below his neck and squeezed the trigger. The gun fired. Over went the bear. The report from the pistol seemed to go on forever. I ran up and stood fifteen feet from him. He was alive long enough for me to say a prayer for his spirit. Then he heaved the infamous "death moan".

In almost every bear story I heard or read, I've heard tell of the "death moan". I always thought it was a myth, until now. I waited to make double-dog sure he's dead, then I headed for the cabin to get the boys. The 250 yards back to the bear went relatively quickly considering two of the three of us had legs shorter than some of the scrubbrush we were walking through.

As we approached the animal I made the boys stand 15 feet up a hill while I rolled him over and posed for a picture. I really thought the picture had a chance of coming out with a seven-year-old operating the manual 35 mm camera. Jake, my oldest, said "Daddy, who's poop is that?" pointing to a pile. All of a sudden I knew why the bear was rocking side to side as I shot. He probably could have used a little Metamucil. Now we know the answer to the age old question "Does a bear shit in the woods?" Not anymore!

After the photo-op I rolled the 300-pound beast on his back, straddled his stomach and began skinning. I put my left palm against his right paw and pushed his arm back. With my right hand I held the Buck knife. As I inserted the blade into the bear's forearm, his claws flexed between my fingers. I don't know if I'll ever feel the shocking terror again that ran through body at that moment.

The flex was just reflex, of course, but if the bear had "come to" it would have been spooky, if not deadly, with an armed buddy standing by.

My heart stopped while I thought of what could happen while my four and seven-year-olds were standing by armed only with their Power Rangers and camera. Once my heart began beating again I finished the task at hand and took the boys back to the cabin.

After carrying the hide to the cabin, I stripped and waded into the creek. The water cooled my core body temperature down to a level no longer able to steam rice as I washed the blood from my skin. I looked to the creek, the trees and the sky and said, "Thank you." I turned to walk out of the water, naked and feeling close to the land, and there on the shore where I've walked 20 times before in the last two days, was the wing feather from a bald eagle. I picked it up, nodding my appreciation to the unseen spirit who had placed it there. Dressed and back in the cabin, I read the kids a bed time story, kissed them goodnight and fell into my bunk. The last thing I did before falling into a deep, dreamless sleep, was place the eagle feather next to my pillow.

From the ocean the Island doesn't look as scary

Forget Your Gun

I seem to remember it being in my early twenties, the first time I "forgot" how old I was. It is such a goofy feeling to forget something so apparently meaningful. I would've never believed it if someone had told me that more than once in my life, while hunting, I would forget that I was carrying a gun. If you've ever heard, "You'd forget your head if it wasn't attached to your neck," the next couple stories will show you why I now check the top of my neck, daily.

When I was 19 I lived in Juneau. My friend Ron invited me to join him deer hunting on

Admiralty Island one November day. Admiralty Island has more brown bears per square mile than any other place in Alaska. On Saturday morning we climbed in his 18-foot Avon inflatable with the twin 35 horse outboards and headed around Douglas Island. We skirted the coast of the North Eastern side of Admiralty until we ended up in Young's Bay. This would be our deer hunting Mecca. I, being a young strapping boy from the eastern flat side of Montana, didn't realize what "lots of deer" also meant in Alaska: "Lots of bears" really like "lots of deer." So as you'd expect, with "lots of deer" come "lots of bear".

We anchored the boat at the tide line and unloaded our gear. Ron explained that in the thin row of spruce trees that lay ahead of us he had constructed a tree stand. Right on the other side of the row of trees was a huge meadow where we thought we might spot a few Sitka blacktail. We approached the treeline very cautiously and looked at the meadow. After about 15 or 20 minutes, Ron leaned his gun against the tree and climbed to the tree stand. When he got to the top, I did the same.

Just as I put my right foot into the structure, I heard a noise down below. As I looked down a movement from under the tree next to us caught my eye. Fifty feet below me was about an eight foot brownie just a sauntering around trying to find whatever stinky thing it was that had woken him up. That, of course, was me. I'm now up the tree without a gun.

I grabbed a pair of binoculars and looked at the beast up close and personal. The bear was walking around very cautiously, sniffing in the air. I thought it would be funny to bark like a dog and watch the startled beast run away not ever knowing what had scared him. I, of course, was young and stupid. The bear's head occupied the entire view through the binoculars. As I did my absolute best canine bark, I even fancied this particular bark to be that of a German shepherd. The bear slowly and methodically turned his head in a kind of rotating fashion and looked straight through the lens and through my eye directly to some secret spot hidden inside my skull where a huge primeval horror always waits for this very moment to arise.

Unlike stories told by World War II or Vietnam snipers about staring down an enemy sniper, scope to scope, before one loses the battle of nerves, my hands began to shake as we had this moment of connection. There was the largest bear I had ever seen standing fifty feet below me, looking me right in the eye. More importantly, my rifle lies closer to him than to me. After the three hours that we stared at each other, okay probably more like five seconds, the bear trotted off in a nervous gait. During the next two days we saw brown bears 14 additional times.

At first light the second morning, I was standing at the edge of a muskeg - a swampy clearing of peatbog found in arctic climates - about a hundred yards across when something caught my eye. In retrospect I realize it was a brown bear dropping from his hind legs to all four. At the time I didn't know what it was, although it began to unfold quickly that the large dark figure approaching me had fangs, claws and appeared to possess a very aggressive disposition.

All I could think of was what Hunter Safety had taught me seven years before: don't run from a predator. I kept repeating to myself, "It's only a bluff, don't run, it's only a bluff, don't pee in your pants, it's only a bluff."

In truth, brown bears can close a 100 yard gap in 5 seconds. It seemed like even less time and the bear was now only 30 feet from me. He stopped, woofed twice like a dog, and pounced sideways toward me. I stood perfectly still. Well, as perfectly still as I could for someone shaking like a 4 hp vibrator sander. The bear ran away a bit, stopped, woofed again, pounced sideways toward me again, then ran off into the woods.

The bear would never be a Boone and Crockett record. He was probably an eight and a half or nine footer, but for a moment or two he seemed much larger.

The woods were almost eerie in the silence that followed. I didn't move for about 10 minutes. A mist hung in patches around the clearing. The setting was too serene. Did that really happen? Did I just make it all up in my head? Everything was way too calm. I started to look for prints, maybe a broken twig, anything that would give truth to my doubting mind. I found nothing. I widened my search until finally I saw it. One print, then another, followed by another. It truly had happened.

I sat down because the adrenaline was getting the best of me. I laid my gun on my lap. It was at that moment that I finally remembered I had a gun. I had totally forgotten during the entire incident. I reached up and checked my neck. It was probably best I didn't remember about the gun. It was only a .22-250. A great deer gun but it probably would have just pissed the bear off if I had shot him. I had a .44 magnum, too, but ballistically it only packs the punch of a .30-30.

They say the best thing you can do if you're going to face a grizzly with a .44 is to carry some lubricated loads and file the front sight off so it won't hurt as much when the bear shoves the pistol up your ass. That's why so many hunters have a strange stride when they return from Alaska hunting excursions. They won't ever tell you the truth. Instead, they'll say they fell off a ladder or rolled an ankle. The truth is they suffered a "Remington enema" from Yogi the bear and they still can't walk correctly. And, if they used bear slugs, it gives them a new meaning for the term "butt plug."

You would think once in a lifetime would be lesson enough. But that wasn't the first time I forgot I was packing heat.

The first time was late 1976. Our country was celebrating its bicentennial. Never before had I seen this country so proud of itself, at least not in all my 13 years. I was just as proud to be taking part in a custom steeped in tradition. That cold November morning, as I dragged myself out of bed at the ungodly hour of 3:30 a.m., I was participating in a father/son deer hunt.

We climbed in the 1964 Scout that was my father's pride and joy. According to dad that Scout, with its 4 cylinder engine, could "climb a telephone pole." With as many times as we got stuck or powered down trying to climb a hill I figured he was probably right. If while you were climbing that telephone pole someone was kind enough to lie the pole on its side, and the wind wasn't blowing too hard in your face and maybe you were actually kind of going down hill at the same time, then, yeah, it probably could climb a telephone pole.

Dad warmed up the "truck," as he called it, before he asked me to climb in. I curled up like a ball in the shotgun seat and pretended to be awake as dad would drive us to our destination.

It was a big deal for the old man, being out on the hunt with his only son. Of course it was a huge deal for me, actually getting to go out and operate on inadequate amounts of sleep, eat soggy egg salad sandwiches, and freeze my little hiney off standing outside on some strategic point that my father picked for me. You know, being a man.

We drove south that morning. Dad said he had a gut feeling that we'd see an enormous Muley buck if we were in the steppe country south of Belfry. I told him that gut feeling was probably gas.

Somewhere after "The Home of the Bats", Belfry's High School mascot, and before the Wyoming state line, we took a left off the highway. In Montana taking a left off the highway doesn't always imply that there's a road to the left, and such was the case here. We followed what started out looking like a faint Jeep trail, but it ended up probably being a cattle trail, until we had gotten as far off the main road as my father felt the Scout could go. This distance, I always felt, should have been cut in half since my dad only has one leg and when we get stuck I was the one that had to hump out for help.

Dad shut off the engine and we sat. Legal shooting time was still an hour off but by God we were in position for when the official moment arrived.

Dad poured himself a cup of coffee from his old green Thermos. It was his last vestige from his more prosperous days as a toolmaker making parts for Boeing. I tried to sleep. About a half hour later he shook me lightly. As I came to, he was pointing out my window.

Out in the dark I could start to make out something moving. As I looked I saw that it was a nice mule deer walking along a game trail. Not only was it a good sized deer, but now I could see it also had an admirable rack. I couldn't tell exactly how many points it had, but both dad and I knew it would go on the wall.

We waited about fifteen minutes until dad said it was legal shooting time and I should head down the game trail. I grabbed the Remington Mohawk 6 mm and opened the door. I didn't fully shut the door as I left because dad taught me better than to make that much noise. I headed down the trail picking up the buck's spoor as the rising sun slowly began illuminating the land with every footstep I took.

I followed his tracks for about thirty minutes, then saw a set of cat tracks coming onto the game trail from the right. I'm not talking about your everyday run of the mill Tabby, either. I'm talking about cat tracks that would cover the tracks of a big dog. This was definitely a cougar, a mountain lion. I had never seen a cougar in the wild before so it kind of excited me. I became even more titillated when I saw the cat's track on top of the buck's track. I knew the buck was less than fifteen minutes ahead of me and I knew the mountain lion was closer than that.

It was a weird, almost bonding feeling, both of us trailing the same prey. I knew at that moment that I was born a predator. Hunting is not a learned behavior; it's a natural nurturable instinct.

The game trail was now at the foot of a rock bench about five or six feet tall. It was a wet morning so tracks on the trail would fill with a little water as soon as they were made. I could turn around and see mine fill in behind me.

As I walked along I thought my mind was playing tricks on me. It seemed the pool in the feline's tracks still had ripples in them. I pushed on, fear rising. It happened again. Did the water move or was it just me? I stopped for a couple seconds then decided this is what happens when your mind is tired.

Then, I saw it...the water WAS still moving in THAT track. I felt the hair on the back of my neck stand up as I looked 20 yards ahead to see the stalking cat perched on top of the bench. It was crouched low and looking straight at me. Suddenly I knew what Jerry the mouse felt like when Tom the cat drank the "Jekyll and Hyde" potion.

I made what could have been a mortal sin in the outdoors. I turned and ran. Looking back now from the hill of maturity the only theory I can offer as to why I'm alive is that cat's reflexes were faster than mine. He must have run the other way before he could see me take off. If he had seen me run, I'm sure he would have been on me in a flash. You've seen cats chase their prey. Wham!

I ran as fast as my stubby little teenage legs could carry me all the way back to the car where dad was waiting. He rolled his window down as I was well into the story about what had just happened. When he figured out what I was rambling about, his first question was, "why didn't I shoot the damn thing?"

I checked my neck but didn't want to admit out loud that it was only that very moment when I remembered I had a gun. So I tried to spin a yarn with an excuse as its main theme. As I worked my way through a whopper of a story I begin to notice a cold sensation in my groin. I look down and sure enough... a pair of Depends would've helped.

I crawled back in the Scout and took off my wet pants, wrapped up in a blanket and we drove off in search of other great reasons to celebrate our nation's 200th anniversary.

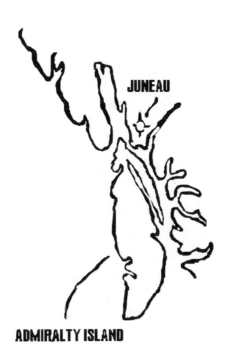

JUNEAU

ADMIRALTY ISLAND

Captain Raymond about to net a Kenai king

Chinook

To fish for kings (chinook salmon - *Oncorhynchus tshawytscha*) on the Kenai river, for a local, is to fish for the world record. The river is home to the world record sport-caught chinook salmon. Les Anderson in 1985 caught the 97 lb. 4 oz. buck at a hole called "The Pillars," not far from the towns of Soldotna and Kenai, Alaska.

The Kenai is the last of its kind, a river with the last un-enhanced run of great kings left in the world. Every time you dip a line into the water between May and August, you have a chance to catch a new world record. Fish and Game says that in any given year there are probably 20 or more fish returning to the Kenai that top the magical 100 lb. mark. Catching the record is, of course, the dream of every angler on the river. In reality catching anything over 50 or 60 lb. is a gift from God. This is the story of one such gift.

It was chilly that July morning as I climbed into the Willie Predator riverboat. Raymond McGuire with Kenai River Guide Service was captain. I had known Raymond for about six years. We were neighbors back in the early 1990s. We had nothing in common, save a love for fishing. We had chased rainbows together for a couple years on the Upper Kenai, but Raymond hadn't caught a king at that point. I remember teaching him to tie an eggloop, a popular hook tie among those of us who regularly chase the elusive chinook.

I was a bit skeptical when he announced that he was beginning his own guide service for kings the year after I taught him to tie the eggloop! But within two years he had caught a local news-breaking 89-pounder for a client.

Raymond hadn't been a guide very long, but he was focused. Some might call Raymond "obsessive", while others call him a "savant". Come to think of it, he does kind of resemble Dustin Hoffman in "Rainman" and I think he buys Fruit of the Looms at K-mart.

Fishing in not-so-traditional holes produced that huge buck. But like I said earlier, Raymond was focused. Raymond didn't drink, chase women or go to church. He fished! He had spent the last three years living, breathing and drinking the life of a Kenai River king guide.

Guides on the Kenai are limited to fishing from a uniform start time of 6 a.m. As the other guides were heading downstream from the Centennial Park launch in Soldotna, we headed upstream. The river is wide here but it has its share of hull splitting rocks and blind, dead-end sloughs, too. Raymond glided the boat through the labyrinth, each bend bringing us that much closer to "the hole".

We arrived at our destination at about 6:25 a.m. and began what is known as back-bouncing our eggs through the hole. Back-bouncing is a method of presenting your bait just a bit slower than the current and with as much control of the bait as humanly possible. It's a great way to hook kings if you know what you're doing!!! As soon as the king starts nibbling, you can sense it. A green hook-setter will invariably rip the hook from the fish's mouth at this point. Only a seasoned angler, you know, one who spends more than his annual salary on outdoor gear for each season, has the patience to wait till the lunker engulfs the bait enough to get a proper hook set.

The third pass over the grounds gave us

a rod-tip slam to the water. "See," said Ray. "You tide fishermen are so narrow minded, 'only fishing the tide'. Third pass up here and we get a big slam!!!" Then, nothing! Some king took a swipe at the cured eggs and apparently thought better. Still it was enough to get your adrenaline pumping so early in the morning. Hell, it makes mine pump like that at noon, too! Come to think of it, a bream or a bullhead makes mine pump, but that's for another story. This was unmistakably a fish over 30 pounds.

We waited, hitless, for another hour, then two hours, then three. Drift after drift, skein after skein. We stopped at noon to have lunch. I suggested moving down to catch the incoming tide since fresh kings would be coming in on the swell. Raymond would not be talked into moving. He almost acted as if I was questioning his abilities as a guide, as a fisherman ... as a man! The suspicious tone he took with me hurt. I'm not saying it wasn't true, I'm just saying it hurt.

Raymond started in again, "You tide fishermen are so close-minded. You think the only fish in this river are the ones coming in on the tide swell, twenty thousand kings projected for this run and you act like they're all coming in on the tide that YOU choose to fish! Ego, Ego, Ego!!!" I conceded. We stayed on "the hole". Well, he made a good argument. He pointed out that it was his boat, and he paid for the gas and he wanted to stay here. Who was I, as a freeloader, to argue?

We drifted again and again. Finally the rod began to bounce a little more than the natural flow of the river bottom would cause. "See! I told you! Only fish the incoming tide! Ha! Ol' Raymond knows this part of the river like nobody!!!" I knew a king was sitting right below the current mouthing the eggs attached to my line. Raymond whispered with anticipation, "Get ready...Get ready..."

Most people think all fish are in a feeding or fighting mode when they get hooked, and in most cases they're probably right. One theory on the kings is that because of their slow, gentle take of the bait (relative to that of a coho), they are actually giving in to a parental instinct. That is to say they are taking the eggs into their mouths to move them out of the current and into an eddy or pool where they can drop to the gravel and hatch. It doesn't explain every hit I get, but it works for some, like this one.

As strong as a German shepherd trying to tear a rag from your hand, the salmon pulled at my line one tug with each headshake. I could visualize the violent tossing, back and forth 15 feet below the surface and about 40 feet behind the stern. I fought off the natural instinct to set the hook and horse him in. This was no pan-sized rainbow or even a burly largemouth. This was a sleeping torpedo about to wake up and try to sink the Bismarck! I let up on the pressure a bit, he calmed down the same degree, still holding onto the bait.

Raymond watched like a golden retriever who just spotted a flock of pheasants. I waited for what seemed to be an eternity, then lowered the Greatlander medium-heavy casting trigger rod tip down to the water, and tightened up the slack. "Cross his eyes!" barked Raymond. Snap! I brought the shaft to my shoulder. The tip barely moved from the waterline.

I was ready for an explosion and was somewhat shocked when it didn't happen. It was as if I had set the hook in a wet, mushy log. I looked at the rod, then looked at Raymond. Raymond looked at me. We both looked at the doubled over rod. Then a shake, then another. I braced myself against the gunwale. The rod pulled me to the side as the silver-finned Patriot missile shot upstream.

Most places I've caught kings, when hooked, they go downstream. The Kenai is usually no exception, unless it's a big one. First, they make a sprint upstream usually ending with a full-bodied leap at the end as if to say "See what you will never have?" Oh, you, as a reader, may dismiss them as "only fish" with no petty emotions like jealousy, petulance or vindictiveness. I tell you though, I've seen them, on the upper Kenai, pointing a dorsal fin at me, swimming right past my lure laughing, with a smile on their face and the look of a teen-age tease in their eyes.

This one took off upstream and leaped. I guessed him to be about seventy pounds by the way he eclipsed the northern hemisphere when he cleared the water. He had a splash roughly the size of a depth charge when he re-entered. Then he quickly cut across the current, changing the position of my rod 90 degrees. The battle had begun. Downstream he ran.

Raymond rowed the boat to assist me in not losing all my line. "Keep on him," he yelled. My Abu Garcia 5503 C reel was only packing a few hundred feet of 20-pound test Maxima "Chameleon." It's a little brittle, but it doesn't stretch much when setting the hook. It does, however, sing when its being peeled off your reel by a slab of fish-flesh propelling itself down a river at 30 miles per hour.

The brute stopped in a hole around the corner, he was just sitting. I let up on the pressure, when he stopped, giving him as much encouragement to stay as I could, until I had gained enough line to feel safe again. He seemed content to stay right there. Unfortunately, it doesn't help to let them sit and rest very long so I reset the hook.

When you battle one of these lunkers for a while, the hook will twist and turn enough to enlarge the jaw-hole in which it sets. Once the hole is bigger than the hook-shaft, the hook can slip out. This is why a re-set is important every so often with big kings.

I gave the rod a couple firm snaps. On the second one, I felt his head shake again and braced for another run. He took off like a shell out of a Howitzer. The reel sang again as the cache of line on my reel shrank. Raymond again frantically rowed to keep up with the run. Out of the water he launched himself again. This time he ran toward a big log jam. It would be a decisive end to the fight if he reached the logs. I thumbed the reel a little and leaned to "head" him out from the bank. It worked. He never reached the timbers.

By the time the third run was over and the 70 pounds of pre-cured lachs was resting again, we were a half-mile downstream from where we hooked the hog. I re-set the hook again but this time the head shakes were slow to respond and fewer in number. I knew the battle was nearly over.

I made the decision to try horsing him in. I told Raymond and he grabbed the oversized net. I began to lift the fish off the bottom. Up he came, begrudgingly, but up nonetheless. We saw color, he gave a couple swooshes of his tail and pulled 10 or 20 feet of line in vain. He was spent. Raymond lowered the net, and said calmly, "Come on in baby. It was a good fight. Time for a long rest." I guided him in. Raymond sat down and grinned at me.

At the scales he weighed in at 67 pounds, a respectable fish, but the only true excitement came from tourists, who gawked, smiled and said, "Hey, there's one for the wall!" The locals just glanced at the fish, glanced at me and walked by unimpressed. After all, we were fishing the Kenai!

Quietly, they appear out of the brush right behind you

Grizzly Bear

Ursus Arctos, or *Ursus Arctos Horribilus*, the animal is more commonly referred to as "grizzly", "Alaskan brown bear" or "brownie." Any way you look at it, stature-wise, it's the largest predator on the North American continent.

I, like most people, feared them. How can you blame me? I had seen the movies and read the stories of the villainous grizzly bears who slink around the thick undergrowth flexing their sharp claws and killing every living thing they come across, including every human they see, in a ferocious, violent attack that most often ends in a blood-dripping muzzle and a defiant roar.

Well, that was then. Now, after seeing literally hundreds in the wild, being face to face with dozens, staring down the rifle at a few, tracking the blood spoor of a couple, being bluff charged by one, and splitting a canoe paddle over the head of an obstinate three-year-old, that fear is now admiration for the gentle giants who are more like a displaced remnant of a long gone era.

In August I had a nonchalant conversation about hunting with Craig Ketchum, owner and proprietor of Ketchum Air. He talked with me about what I was going to do to top the black bear I shot in July. Would it be a record caribou, a moose, or maybe, he suggested, a goat in Prince William Sound. I said they all sounded great but what I really wanted was a brownie.

He said he had seen a big one the fall before digging a den through the snow near Beluga Lake. We decided that's where it was going to be and I picked Labor Day for the start of a week long hunt.

My hunting partner on this trip would be Dave Denslow. He was the 'fish guy' at Knights Taxidermy in Anchorage. We headed out on Saturday and had a wonderful evening setting up bear camp. Our pilot, Con, who later served in the Alaska State Legislature as a senator, dropped us off in the northwest corner of the lake. There was a cove there with a perfect place for camp about 100 yards south of the inlet creek.

As we set up camp I promised Dave we would see a bear in the cove. That night we speared a salmon and cooked it up for dinner. After dinner we walked the creek bed. We saw bear sign all over the creek. We marked what was 'old' by placing white stones on the piles. Since all of the piles consisted of blueberries, crowberries, or currents it was easy to tell where our hunting prospects would be best.

The next morning we got up, made breakfast and went for a scouting trip looking for the berry patch. We walked due south until we came to the Triumvirate Glacier run-off river. We glassed the valley for a while until I saw movement. I told Dave to look across the valley. At the ridge line something small and black was moving along quite rapidly. It was too small to be a black bear. I figured it must be a porcupine, or if we were lucky, maybe a wolverine. Dave decided to go in search of the great black figure. I agreed to sit on my butt, keep an eye on it and direct him from above. It took him about 20 minutes to get to the other side. Then about 15 minutes later he shot once, twice, three times.

I could see him start back and decided to do a little exploring while I waited. I went up the rocks until I came to the top of a natural, but crude, stair step formation. I worked my way through some alder bushes to find the mother of all berry patches. Blueberry and crowberry bushes stretched as far as the eye could see. Walking across them felt like walking on bubblepack from the Post Office. You could actually feel the berries pop under each step.

When Dave returned he showed me the dead porcupine in the pack and I told him about my find. We agreed to hunt the patch tomorrow.

We walked back to camp and prepared dinner. The camp felt rather loose that evening. We were being quite noisy and had a big fire burning. At one point, about 9 p.m., I told Dave that I was going to cut some branches off the tree so I could see the cove from my chair. He took that as his cue to start skinning his porcupine. After I cut the tree branches, the bush beyond it was still in my way. I decided to cut it down too. With my back to the cove I began to cut. When I finished I stepped back and could see my chair perfectly through the hole in the foliage. Then I turned to look at the cove.

Across the other side was a bear walking the shore. The size and shape of the head was the first indication that it was a brownie. I sprinted the 20 yards to my rifle. Dave didn't need to be told what was happening, he knew by the speed I was moving. He ran for his gun, too. As I arrived at the cove shore the bear had just walked behind some tall grass across the water. I dove into a cut out in the bank, almost like a natural foxhole. Dave jumped in. When the bruin came back out of the grass it was looking straight at us.

We had a perfect view through our scopes as the bear stopped and sat on its hind legs only 120 yards away. Dave whispered to me, "It's not the biggest brownie, but it's not bad. You gonna let it go?" I replied "No. I'm gonna take it." Boom! The report of the .338 rang as the bear spun to the right. Then, it showed it's broadside and Dave let one fly from his 30.06. The bear slowly walked about six yards and fell over.

We spent the next 10 minutes collecting the gear we'd need, including a lantern and flashlights because darkness was fast approaching. When we got to the bear it was still breathing. I stopped at 30 feet, put the cross hairs of my rifle scope at the base of her head and squeezed. With the bear now across the river Styx we posed for a couple photos and skinned it out. Turned out to be about a four year old sow. We were back in camp by 11 p.m., celebrated by having a Mountain Dew and got to sleep with both of us clutching our pistols.

We still had five days left in bear camp and Dave still wanted to bag a blackie. The next day as we were out for a walk we spotted a sow black bear and two cubs on the far south buttress of the berry patch. We sat and watched them for about half an hour, then continued our walk. We returned to camp to set over the carcass for the evening. On Tuesday we went back to the south buttress and watched the three bears again for a while. We even took quite a few snapshots. Then we decided to go and hunt the northwest quarter of the patch.

Just as we started into that quadrant I saw a huge brown shape about 400 yards ahead. It was just like the cover of National Geographic with the fall colors of the sparsely treed tundra. The Alaska Range rose up above the glaciers all less than a mile away and between us was the patriarch of the wilderness. The great Alaskan brown bear, a 10-footer easy, maybe even 11. (See scratch marks in photo.) Dave came up behind me sneaking from bush to bush. It was obvious he had seen it, too.

We stalked up another 200 yards to a spot where we could see the bear clearly. Dave knelt down to get ready. He took position, aimed and squeezed the trigger. The massive beast spun around and ran quartering away from us. Dave got off a couple more shots but the bear was running like Seattle Slew. It was our worst nightmare, a wounded bear. We had no option, we had to find him.

It took two hours before we finally found his spoor. The blood trail was not easy to follow with two drops here and one drop there. We followed it, always one eye on the trail, the other looking for a pissed-off bear who may very well now be tracking us. The bushes were high, the tundra was difficult to traverse, and it took another hour of exhausting searching until we busted out of the bushes into the creek. We hoped he had turned and gone either up or down the creek because on the other side was nothing but alder bushes. But the signs told us otherwise. That damned bear had done the smart thing. The trail went right through the alders. Dave stepped right up and said it was his bear so he should go first. I agreed.

Have you ever tried to track a dangerous, wounded grizzly bear through thick alders? Your first thought is that there is no way an animal of that astounding bulk can walk through alders this thick. Wrong. When a bear goes through alders the bushes part like the Red Sea. When a man goes through, he crawls, laboriously, clothes hanging up on twigs, vision obscured by the maze of twisted branches.

It's amazing how loud your heartbeat is when your life depends on how quiet you can be. Not that I think I can be quiet enough to sneak up on any animal. I was trying to be quiet so I could hear anything moving or breathing or blinking an eyelash. Things feel a bit tense when you're crawling on your hands and knees following the blood dripping from an 1,100 pound pissed off brown bear that you couldn't see if he were 10 feet in front of you.

We followed the blood about 300 yards through the thicket, crawling and cursing, to a spot where it appeared the bear had laid down to lick his wound. There was no blood leaving the site so we circled around for awhile trying to find anything. We found nothing. With no more sign we had to assume he stopped bleeding. We clambered around the bushes for about two hours. Nothing. No blood, no prints, nothing. It was getting dark, and I remember thinking things couldn't get much worse. Then the rain came and proved me wrong. We couldn't do any more this day, so we left, wet, exhausted and discouraged.

It was a gentle rain, but it kept falling, relentlessly, for the next five days. Every morning, the same routine, crawl out of the tent, eat breakfast, and search for sign of the bear. Back to camp by nightfall, tired and sore from pushing through thickets looking for a print, a blood trail, anything to lead us to a wounded animal. We retraced our tracks through the alders; we scoured the berry patch and walked the creek bed every day. The rain wasn't helping as it slowly erased all tracks and signs.

The last day came and as we tore down camp there was a sour taste in our mouths. To put your mind to rest, it wasn't my cooking that caused it. If you hunt long enough, you will eventually run into a situation where a wounded animal escapes. In hindsight, maybe we should have tried to get closer. Maybe I should have offered Dave my .338 to use instead of his 30-06. I don't know. I do know you never want to leave an animal without knowing what happened to it. But try as we might, we never knew. Even as the floatplane circled up after take-off, my eyes were still searching for him. Nothing. We headed back to town.

The wounded grizzly weighed heavy on my mind that winter, and I relived the hunt often in my mind, wondering if we could have done more to see if he had lived or died. The next spring I made a couple attempts to return to the area to look for signs, but to no avail. The plans never materialized. I did make it back in the fall though, one year to the week of the initial hunt. As I walked the shore of the lake, I came upon a fresh set of huge tracks in the mud of the cove. A slow smile crossed my face. Bears are territorial, and when

a bear that big stakes out his territory, other big bears either challenge him to the death, or move out to claim their own kingdom. I'm pretty sure our bear was still there. Seeing his tracks made me feel a whole lot better.

How a brownie says, "Here's my territory. Here's how big I am."

In the day the anchor always holds. That night however...

December Deer

The snow and sleet were pelting the left side of my face at 70 knots. It really stung. I knew how fast because I had noticed the winds speed earlier while I was still in the cabin. I was sure hypothermia was already setting in. It was Alaska's December cold and I was dripping wet and alone on the island.

I was underwater just 10 minutes before, in the North Pacific. Beneath my thin raingear was a pair of cut-off sweat pants and a cotton T-shirt, both saturated with icy seawater. At least I was wearing knee high neoprene boots; too bad they were also soaked and providing me no comfort. You always read about guys dying dressed like this and wonder why they didn't know better.

When the anchor broke free, and the boat began to drift again, I was being drug, heels first, though large stones that comprised the rough, jagged ice-coated beach. The combination of ice and frozen rocks had the same delicate feel upon my face as 80 grit sandpaper. I strained to look through the blizzard, towards the deck, and saw Jake, my 17-year-old son looking back. If I lost the rope or the other end slipped from the cleat on the boat, this would be the last time he would see Dad until they found my cold, blue, lifeless body the next day, if at all.

Captain Dudley yelled out to me "Don't let go, I won't be able to get back to find you." I was pulling hard against the rope, the boat just kept moving out to sea, my heels were cutting deep trenches in the beach and I was getting closer and closer to the frosty water.

I wondered, "How in the Hell did I get here?"

The trip had been planned, hell almost expected, for nearly a year. I had the week before Christmas scheduled off work, we were just waiting for the right weather and it opened just in time. This would be our second late December deer hunt in as many years together.

Dudley was the owner of a local power sports/mining supply company. We had known each other for almost 20 years, but had only in recent years started hanging out together. We took our sons on this hunt. Jake, my 17-year-old and Michael, his 15-year-old, were both exceptional students and accomplished athletes at the newest high school in town. The athlete part can be duly noted by Jake's State Championship football ring and Michael's State Championship soccer ring.

We had to tow the boat, first by road, then through a one-lane tunnel, to the small harbor hamlet of Whittier, Alaska. About 300 residents live in Whittier. It's located on the western edge of Prince William Sound and was established during World War II as a military supply port. It still looks like it in an abandoned kind of way.

We filed our "float-plan" with the harbormaster and left about midday. The sun's not up for very long mid-winter so midday is only a few hours 'till dark in Alaska in December. It was a calm ride out the first night and we made it to an anchorage in West Twin Bay at Perry Island just in time to see the sun set and cook an early 4 p.m. dinner.

The snow was falling fairly hard when we woke the next morning. That was promising. Snow drives deer down to lower elevations on the islands in Prince William Sound and if it was heavy snow, the deer seek out the beaches. This would be the ultimate situation as the more deer on the beach made the chances of seeing deer better. Seeing deer really was a key part in reaching our goal, for this was planned as a Montague Island deer-hunting trip.

The boat was made with Alaska in mind. A 26-foot Kingfisher Pilot House aluminum-hulled cabin cruiser with twin Honda 130s off the swim platform. It cut the four foot rollers well. The trip from Perry Island to where we were headed took a few hours. It would have taken less but we stopped by a secret fishing hole, well, a not so well known fishing "spot" near Naked Island which Dudley and Michael had discovered a few years ago while boating during the summer.

Prince William Sound is a large and expansive sound full of islands, coves, bays, and passages. It takes only two days to cross the sound but a lifetime could be spent exploring it all. A geographical map only gives you part of the story. You really need a chart so as to see the underwater topography and to really understand the fishing opportunities that abound. Underwater troughs, pinnacles, and plateaus tell quite a tale to those versed in its piscatorial language.

This spot, while not often used, always produced fish, lots of fish. This day was no exception. We only stopped for a few minutes, dropping heavy jigs to the bottom at 70 fathoms, then reeling a couple feet off the bottom on a drift across the "hole." This method produced three nice little chicken halibut.

Anything weighing less than 20 pounds is referred to as a "chicken" in Alaska. Big halibut, weighing in over 80 pounds, are caller "shooters", because we shoot them with either a pistol or a .410 snake charmer to stop them from destroying our boats. Anything over 200 pounds are simply referred to as "barn doors." We shoot "barn doors," too.

After boating our dinner, the journey continued with me outside on the deck filleting the chickens, somewhat of a challenging job in rough seas, but I got it done. It was probably done more quickly and poorly so as to not stay out in the cold any longer than I had too. We headed southeast and made it to Gilmour Bight, a long, but narrow inlet just north of Port Chalmers on Montague Island, around 3 p.m. It was good timing as the storm was getting more intense and the seas were getting higher. We had plenty of light and huntable terrain, but the storm was really blowing.

Near the head of the bight, we set two anchors, one off the bow and the other off the stern, to try and keep the sway to a minimum and chose the morning to hunt since it was forecast calm.

Dudley is somewhat of a gourmet chef and began to cook a dinner surpassing most five star restaurants in Alaska. His plans went a little astray when he noticed that I forgot to get the garlic. I took out the list he gave me and showed him that nowhere on it was the word "garlic" or 'garlic cloves," but in the end agreed that since this was not the first time I had the pleasure of his cooking and since we were all garlic-a-holics, that I should have known to bring some, regardless. He still pulled off a dish of fish that was delectable.

For hours we sat playing Texas hold 'em and telling the kids "when we were your age" tales. We chatted about South Anchorage High and sports until well after the sun set around 4 p.m. By that time the clouds were so thick, it was really more of a dimming until dark. Nighttime wintry fog in Alaska produces an eerie backdrop. There was no sky, no stars, no light whatsoever to keep our bearings. It was as dark as coal in every direction.

By 5 p.m. the wind had kicked up a bit. We finally gave up on the stern anchor idea. We were swinging side to side way too much while the rear continued dragging along. The double anchor method usually works well in light to moderate winds, but when they get to the threshold of "gale force" the second anchor line is just something to get tangled with in the water. Dudley and Jake took the inflatable skiff down the line and pulled the rear anchor, then returned to the game at hand.

About 7:30, after going "all in" and winning with a pair of pocket aces, I made a stunning observation of which I said out loud, "Dudley, we're dragging anchor at 7 knots." He looked at the GPS display. "Wow, we are!" he said, "All right, lets reposition and re-set the anchor". All hands made ready to move our vessel.

The GPS read the wind blowing from the head of the bay directly out to sea. It was a very tight harbor and the electronics really didn't help our orientation much, so Dudley figured we could slowly follow the anchor line until it was taut, pull the anchor, and just motor forward from that point to shallower water, which would also provide less wind, kind of tucking up under the trees for a windbreak. Good in theory.

We motored forward, directly into the wind. We didn't rush because we were trying to use the anchor line as our point of reference to our position in the cove. As soon as we were on top of the anchor, we should've been able to pull it, increase throttle while moving forward a hundred feet or so, set the pick, and be secure for the night.

The funny thing about great plans is the unexpected consequence. When a boat is at anchor, it's pointed directly in to the wind, meaning the wind is keeping it pointed in that direction by the boat pulling against the anchor line. It's a conflict of design to accomplish a goal. Release the pull of the anchor and half of that equation is gone; therefore the whole practical application is null and void. It's kind of like the old adage, "a kite is only a kite when it's tethered by a string; otherwise, its only trash in the wind."

I don't really know if that is an old adage. I may have just made it up. Regardless, you get the picture. All of a sudden, we were just trash in the wind.

We were 'kiting' either left or right, and we were no longer pointed directly into the 70 knot wind, which just so happened to be the wind speed the GPS was reading. We were most likely pointed in the opposite direction. In this particular instance we couldn't even tell since it was ultra black, no sky, no light on the water, no light on the land; we had nothing with which to orient ourselves to our surroundings. It was reminiscent of playing Marco Polo without the "Polo" echo to help us know where the rest of the players were.

One thing we did know was Prince William sound is not the most charted water on earth and since most of the charts were written before the earthquake of '64, the whole damn seafloor was likely much different compared to what the charts said existed prior to that historic quake. The rocks at the head of the bay appeared more numerous than what we saw in the half light upon entering the bight a few hours and a few feet difference in tide ago.

The Kingfisher was an aluminum-bottomed boat, BUT aluminum only offers a second or two more protection from sharp rocks than fiberglass when the passengers and crew are lodged on top in a big storm. And those rocks were at the entrance to the bight, where the water was deep and the waves were bigger.

We had radar but these conditions made it pretty useless. The storm and the land were one big blob on the screen. Dudley tried to position us as best he could while inside the cabin using the GPS screen. But by the time the signal went up to space, and back down again, it was too old to use. The depth finder kept showing us in increasingly deeper water and every time we thought we were headed in the direction of shallow water, it would only get deeper again.

Of course, in retrospect, and hind site is always 20/20, when we would finally get headed in the right direction, which was directly into the wind, traveling towards the head of the cove and the protection of the trees, the blowing wind would "kite" the bow around toward the shore and eventually directly towards the sea and the hull splitting rocks again. For every ten feet we made it to shore we sailed 20 or more feet out.

Time really slowed waaayyyy down.

We finally decided to drop anchor again to get the bow headed back into the wind and try to start all over. I climbed forward and gave directional signals with my hand as Dudley let the anchor down. When it finally hit bottom though, the boat just kept on drifting. It was apparent that the bottom was only loose rocks the size of baseballs and footballs. We could not get the anchor to even slow us down. We had traveled far enough down the shoreline to be in the direct path of the full gale, 70 knots of sustained wind with nothing to shield us.

There was a sudden bump. A series of thoughts run rapidly through your head when you feel a bump in a boat. It could have been those sharply pointed rocks that had been ever present in our minds. It could have been a whale. It may have been a floating log. When I looked off the stern, as strange as it seemed at the time, I was somehow relieved to see the rock-strewn beach. The stern had hit into the beach and caused the bump. That's when the panic set in.

Rocks and a stern really don't go together very well. The good news was that the beach slowed our drift down enough for the anchor to bite; unfortunately we were also hung-up on the rocks with the back of the boat. The anchor was trailing behind, the bow was pointed out to sea and the stern was taking the brunt of the wind but it couldn't rotate to face the wind because it was caught up in the rocks and that was the direction it had to spin to set us free. If we could get the stern to clear or even slide over the rocks, the boat would position itself, bow into the wind and in effect, directly toward the head of the cove, where there was less wind and relative safety. That seemed like a far off reality at that moment.

We tried just about everything we could think of to free the back end of the boat, but we were too far in the shallows. We tried to free the anchor to give us enough slack to float into a bit deeper water so we could get the motors up, but when we pulled the line, it was stuck hard. The starboard corner of the stern was at the waterline. The swim platform was hanging over the beach by a few inches. It seemed as if we were going to be there awhile when Dudley said we should tie off to the shore. We'd get beat to hell all night on the beach, but we would not go out to sea and end up on the bigger rocks in deeper water.

Someone had to go ashore with a line and tie us off. I surmised that I was the best qualified, so I stepped through the door to the swim platform, turned and leaned back over the gunwale to grab a line, and stepped off the corner at the beach.

Today, I still don't know if it was the shock of the beach not meeting my feet or the icy seawater covering my body which shocked me the most. The boat had obviously moved a bit while I was looking for the line and when I stepped off, the beach was no longer there to meet my feet. The darkness, alleviating the use of sight, is also deceptive to perceiving movement of a boat, I found out.

I swam a stroke or two to get to solid ground and climbed to shore soaking wet. Dudley yelled to tie off to something. I looked around. The only thing I made out in the dark was a dim tree line about 50 feet away. I ran on the rocks with the line in my hand until I ran out of slack. I was still 20 feet away from the trees and I didn't have enough line to reach.

Dudley was holding the other end of the line and was still on the deck. The waves must have finally rocked the boat enough to free the anchor because it began to drift, bow first toward the ocean. As I followed down the shore, the anchor must have caught again because the boat began to swing around now that it was in deeper water with the bow facing the wind. It seemed like where we wanted the boat to be positioned so we could make a run into the wind to get back to the head of the cove. The only problem in our way was I wasn't on the boat anymore.

The boat began to swing out into deeper water and further away from me. I pulled hard on the line and at one point almost pulled Dudley overboard as he was still holding on to the other end. When that pull swung the boat a little bit towards shore, it gave him just enough slack to slip the loop end around a stern cleat. Now it was just me attached to the boat by my steely kung-fu grip on a 30-foot dock line.

The anchor began to slip again and the boat was drifting out to sea when the realization hit me that if I lost my grip, I was a goner. I dug my heals in and braced to try and stop the boat. For the first time, I noticed how bad I was already shaking from the cold. My knees were like a cartoon character's legs right after he was hit by a falling anvil. I saw this as my heels were carving trenches as the drift of the boat drug me through the rocks. I saw Jake on the stern looking at me. I think it was then that he first realized the situation was not all peaches and cream. I had lost that feeling long ago.

I could hear as Dudley was barking orders to Michael and Jake, desperately trying to make something positive happen. I could barely see the boat when my heels finally hit something solid. It was a boulder and it wasn't going to move. I gave a tug with what seemed like a little more than all my might. At first, the boat would not yield; unwillingly I compressed a bit more. It got to the point of going over the rock or ...hell, I was going over the rock with my feet below me or going over the rock with my feet behind me. I was not letting go.

I have to assume the wind had a slight change because at that moment, there was a slight reprieve from the pressure tearing my shoulders from their sockets. Then there was a relaxation of the tension. The boat was getting clearer and bigger in my view. It seemed to be swinging my direction for the moment. I reefed on the rope taking up all the slack she would give me.

When the boat was at ten or twelve feet I decided to make my move. It wasn't going to get any closer, so I dove. Bone chilling doesn't truly describe the water of Alaska in December, especially late December. It literally sucks the strength from your body. I managed three haphazard strokes and reached out for the swim platform on the third. Thank God I felt it because I was sapped. I had to rest for a moment to gather enough strength to even pull myself out of the water. Well, Dudley and Jake reached down to help too or I may not have made it.

Once on deck, I knew I had to warm up or my struggle wasn't over. I shook into the cabin, stripped all the soaking clothes off. Well okay, both the sweats and the t-shirt, and dove into the sleeping berth where my, and a few other, sleeping bags were. I don't know if I have ever shaken so violently as I did for the next 20 minutes or so.

As I lay buried under the dry cloth I listened to the action up top. Dudley was calling off water depth, which didn't sound good as it was like hearing a bingo game being called. Numbers came with no regular pattern for a little while except that they kept increasing in value.

The drift had obviously taken us closer to the mouth of the cove where it was much wider. Dudley told Michael that the GPS was finally able to help our orientation to where we were in the cove. He said we were in the middle and told Michael to go to the bow and point directly into the wind. He said keep your arm directly into the wind no matter what direction it comes from.

I believe that was the decision that leads to you being able to read this story from my perspective and not the Coast Guard's assumptions of what may have happened.

The conversation between Dudley and Michael for the next 15 minutes was loud and curt, at least on Dudley's side. That was the only side I could hear from under the four sleeping bags. But the tenseness in his voice eased as the howling of the wind against the structure of the pilothouse eased. Toward the end, he was calling out the depth, in a calm normal voice, in single digit numbers and finally, at 5 feet, he dropped the anchor. It caught right away.

Not that the wind had died yet. He had maneuvered the boat to the head of the cove, tucked in nicely next to the Sitka spruce trees, which blocked a lot of the wind from shoving our boat. The lack of direct assault by the winds and the smaller angle of the anchor line in the shallows allowed the crew to finally get a hold of the bottom with the anchor. It stuck.

Dudley set the anchor alarm on the GPS to notify us if we started to drift again. About 20 minutes later I finally stopped shaking, got dressed and joined them in the cabin for a game of cribbage. Not ten minutes would pass before one of us would be looking at the GPS for comfort. We were looking to make sure there was no drifting involved again.

We relived the exercise through which we had just lived countless times throughout the evening. The two boys drifted off to sleep about midnight. I did shortly after. I don't think Dudley slept until 4 a.m.; at least that's what he claimed when I asked the next morning.

We had a breakfast, took the skiff to shore split up in father/son pairs and began to look for deer. Jake and I went left, or seaward, while Michael and Dudley went right, or inland.

It was a very calm day and there was no snow at the elevations we were hunting, so the outlook for deer was diminished. After walking in a great arc, Jake and I found our way out to the beach. We came out of the trees, I have to imagine, very close to the spot where I must have been standing, soaking wet and cold, the night before.

It gave us a chance to reflect on that moment the night before when he looked out to the beach and saw me fighting to stay connected and alive. He asked if it was scary. I told him that it was. He said he had started to get scared at that moment, too. I told him it was his first "brush." He asked, "Brush with death?" I replied, "or brush with life! Either way, that was your first brush."

We began walking back towards the skiff. Before long I stopped, looked back and assessed the beach where I almost lost my life to machismo, hubris, desperation and stupidity. Could I have survived the night, wet, cold and alone on shore? How many others had faced the same situation

while on remote hunting trips in Alaska, and how many would not return to tell the tale. I viewed the tree stand one last time.

We all got back to the boat empty handed. We drove the shoreline slowly glassing until the time was getting late and made the run for Whittier while we still had enough daylight.

As we were driving home I thought back about the spot on the beach after having seen it in daylight. There was sufficient shelter between the boulders and all the trees. There was certainly a lot of moss for bedding and cover. I suppose I would have stood a chance if I could have gotten out of the wet clothes and gathered enough dry moss and hunkered down behind a big rock or a thick stand of trees. They would have found me with dry moss covering my naked body as I stood to greet them, but I might have lived.

Naw, that visual was too much. I was glad I made it back into the boat. For my reputation's sake alone, I was glad.

Even looking out the back of the cabin, it still looked cold

Brown bears, black bears, and us people, we all come for one of these

"Save Him!" They Say

As a guide, it's a funny thing; you get to take people to some of the most beautiful places in the world. It truly is a once in a lifetime experience for each and every one of them. It was for the guide once, as well. But as I have said in response to that statement more than once, "It's a once in a lifetime trip, unless you make it 70 times per year and it's your tenth year going!

After that amount of time you do get a collection of stories to tell. They, too, are great and entertaining as hell, even the seven hundredth time you get to tell them. It's mostly entertaining though to see and hear the responses.

In 1991 I was working part-time as a guide for a local fly-out air service. There was a "fish dry spell" in the areas we flew from the second week of June through early July and I think that was why I was elected to be the guinea pig guide for a new place for sockeye salmon.

I showed up to work that Saturday morning like any other and awaited instructions on how many clients I would have and where we would be going. We had places to go for rainbows, king salmon, and northern pike this time of year, so the species weren't too many from which to choose. Later would come reds, the pinks and chum and the season would usually wrap up with pike again.

I have to say that that day, June 12, I hadn't been prepared for hearing the words reds (sockeye salmon.) And I had two clients. I looked quizzical, the reassurance came "Yes, I said reds. You're going to Red Salmon Creek." I nodded and left for the gear shed and loaded up on streamer flies and lead weights.

I went and met my guests for the day, explained to them what we were headed out for and told them Red Salmon Creek was our destination, only an hour's flight on our de Havilland Beaver on floats. Now mind you, I had no idea where we were going. I just kind of surmised that it would be somewhere within an hour flight 'cause that's all the further we flew for day fishing.

I watched the terrain and direction as we flew down the west side of Cook Inlet. I saw the Lewis and the Theodore Rivers pass by. I saw Beluga Lake off in the distance. I saw the native village of Tyonek. I watched as we flew over and past some of the over a dozen drilling platforms in the inlet and then I saw the West Forelands. We passed the Kustatan River and headed toward Lake Clark pass.

At the head of the pass, we began our descent and I saw a milky white lake. I wasn't sure of the name but it was definitely a glacier-fed lake, evidenced by its aquamarine turquoise color and the milky white color at the headwaters from all the glacial silt.

I was dropped off in a cove at the west end of the sizable lake and when we were tied off the clients were walked off the back of the floats onto the land. We took the gear and the plane left us for the day. It would be off to other destinations, ferrying clients all around Alaska's backcountry before it returned around five or six to pick us up.

It wasn't difficult to figure out the lay of the water and the fish 'cause they were stacked in the creek's mouth like cordwood. The difficulty

was how to bring a fly through without snagging one every single cast.

About mid-day I invited the clients over to the north side of the cove to sit on some big rocks overlooking the water and broke out the box lunches we provided clients. We all sat for a long time eating and talking about Alaska and where they were from.

A noise from up the creek stopped me in mid-sentence. I looked up the creek and saw a sow black bear and two newborn cubs. I was guarded, but not nervous, as they were a good 50 feet away and didn't seem overly interested in us. We watched as the sow caught a fish and began to eat. The cubs sat and watched and eventually nosed in on the action until she was frustrated with them, walked away leaving them her fish just to start the process over again. We watched as they did this over and over again for about 45 minutes until, as quickly as they had come, they left back up the creek and vanished into the trees.

For the two gentlemen from Indiana, It was the highlight of their Alaska adventure. It was pretty cool for me, too, but I acted cool, as if I had been doing that all my days.

Eventually the plane returned, we picked three fresh dime bright silver fish out of the creek by hand, cleaned them, tossed them in a bag and boarded for the ride back to the dock and Lake Hood.

The next trip out there was just as eventful, although I had three clients to entertain, but the bears came, the fish were everywhere and it was another sunny day in Alaska's rugged backcountry. Magnificent!

It was becoming a regular spot, this Red Salmon Creek. I went out yet a third day. This trip was with two fly fishermen from England. I was sure they were going to have a wonderful trip, just as the last two groups had experienced. We left the dock in the morning and landed around 8:30 a.m. It was cloudy and cool in town when we left, but when we were ten miles out, the sky opened up and you could tell it was going to be another postcard, picture perfect day.

We unloaded, as always, off the back of the floats onto the southern shore. The plane left and we proceeded to the mouth of the creek. The two Brits were feeling just cheeky about all the fish they were catching and releasing.

I judged we had been there around two hours when I heard a noise from the creek. I turned to see a sow black bear, then one, then a second cub in tow. I urged my clients to wade out into the lake so that we could witness this National

Geographic moment of the bears foraging and feeding in their natural habitat. We waded out about 40 feet, within a couple inches of the top of our hip waders, and watched in amazement.

The sow caught fish, the cubs bayed in protest until she caved in and shared, she went to catch another, ate for a few minutes until they noticed and began the begging all over again. This process continued for nearly 20 minutes until I heard a noise from my left.

It was a loud kind of snort that caused my head to spin. As I was drawn towards the movement, I saw a large, not huge, but definitely big brown bear leaping off the rocks toward the blackies. In a split second the sow turned and ran straight back up the creek with one cub right on her heels. They were gone in less than a second.

The other cub didn't run, instead it climbed. It climbed right up the trunk of an old dead tree. It was amazing to see how fast this less-than-a-year-old cub could maneuver vertically. Like a cat on a carpeted pole lying on flat ground, the cub was at the top and cradled in the "y" of the upper-most limbs.

All of this must have happened in a matter of a couple seconds because the griz was nowhere near any of the three when they made their escape. He was, however, at the base of the tree about the same time the cub reached the top. He was bouncing on his front paws, like my English setter bounces when I am holding a doggy treat, staring almost straight up at what I am sure he saw as a noontime snack.

Right away, the cub began to bawl for its mother with a loud, rather obnoxious bawl. A kind of high-pitched, yet guttural loud bray. The brownie backed away from the tree, looked up again and began to circle the tree in a clockwise rotation, all the while grunting and snorting, somewhat reminiscent of an older, mouth breathing trailer dwelling, beer swilling, overweight suspender wearer, who is snoring while in an alcohol induced nap by 2 p.m. after a big morning of drinking.

We backed up into deeper waters to the point where our boots were at their limits. Otherwise the griz would have been no further than five feet from us in his circling. As it was, he was no more than 15 feet from us at the nearest point of his circling. Fortunately for us, he was fixated on the top of the tree and the kibbles that sat in the crotch of the limbs. He circled the tree four or five times. It was a bit of adrenaline that coursed though my veins that makes me not sure of the exact count.

Obviously he had a change of heart on strategy for lunch. He walked directly at the tree trunk, placed one paw on the tree about shoulder height and gave what looked like a little test shove. Then he brought up the other paw right next to it and rocked his body in an effort to push the tree. I chuckled in my head. That was a pretty tough tree and I was certain he couldn't make more than a negligible amount of movement by pushing such a massive old chunk of wood, much less knock it down.

That's where my naivety shows. Bears are deceptively powerful animals. Eventually the tree trunk started rocking. The sway was only slight at the base, but after a minute or two, the upper branches were really showing some travel. The cub never stopped crying for its mother to come back and protect it. The first break in the rhythm of the bawling came when the cub slipped his grip from the now-violent rocking caused by the grizzly at the bottom of the tree. As soon as he regained his grip, the bawling began again, only this time it seemed to have a more urgent tone.

The tree probably only swayed back and forth twice more, when the cub lost its grip all together. The tree launched it through the air like a spring and the cub flew in a cartwheel motion.

Almost as it hit the ground, the brownie was on top with both massive paws and in between, the bears muzzle bit squarely into the small, football sized black bear. The bawling had stopped.

The grizzly bear raised its head, turned towards us, and with blood dripping from its muzzle, it let out what seemed like a defiant roar. We stood, captivated by that which we had just borne witness to.

I realized that my legs were shaking as I stood there. I watched as the boar took the cub's carcass in its mouth, lifted it from the ground like a rag doll and walked slowly into the brush at the south corner of the cove. I could no longer see him or the dead cub.

Peter, the more talkative of the Brits spoke up and said, "That was brilliant! Absolutely brilliant!" I jumped in shock. I had forgotten there was anyone with me until he spoke. Doug, his partner, commented that he should have taken his camera out and taken photos because no one back home would believe them when they told this story.

He's probably right.

Then the crunching noise began. The sound of bones cracking as they were being chewed up by a set of jaws which can deliver over 200 foot pounds as it grinds the bones into manageable size. The griz could be heard crunching for the next two hours.

We actually didn't fish much the rest of the trip, but when the plane came to pick us up, we walked up the creek, eyes to the left the whole time, lifted three fish each out of the water, gutted them and tossed them into our bags.

After I told the story at work, we decided we should try a different tactic to guiding at Red Salmon Creek. Craig, the owner decided that we would need some sort of escape path from the frequent visits from the bruins.

For the next couple of years, we took blue rafts along with us in the plane, unloaded on a sort of floating island of vegetative mat, which could mostly support our weight, blow up the rafts and paddle over to the creek. This way, when the bears came to visit, we could float out a bit and watch.

The next season, we took the rafts out on the first trip and left them on the floating mat, that way they were there whenever we showed up. It worked fairly well in June, July and most of August. Late that month, we jumped into the plane and flew to the lake. We circled the landing area noticing there were lots of little blue things floating in the water over most of the lake. Yes, it was what remains of our rafts after the bears had gotten curious about them. We were stuck back on the shore.

The next year, we took out aluminum boats. They were little ten footers, but held up to bear curiosity much better than plastic.

In the years that followed, that truly became one of my most popular stories to recall as I sat with clients during the times of the day when there were no bears to look at.

The look on their faces was always the same. But the last response was different. If it were a boatload of guys, or outdoorsy gals, they would respond with "Ooo's" and "Aww's."

But if there was a woman, from the city, the response was always the same. When I said "the bears muzzle bit squarely into the small, football sized black bear. The bawling had stopped." They almost invariably said, and in a very firm tone, "Why didn't you save him?" It usually only took a few minutes for them to realize the folly in their questions.

I guess now that I have told the story literally hundreds of times, I am a little shocked why no one asked me why didn't I take any pictures with the camera I had. That, too, would only take a few moments to realize the folly in their question.

What a way to wake up from a nap

The Sound of Completion and Advil!

I had read the outdoors writers of *Field & Stream* ever since I was a young boy in Montana and Idaho. Dreams of incredible adventures chasing wildlife filled my head from the time before I was even a teenager, but one thing I had always read about didn't come into focus until I was much older - the sound of completion.

Different authors wrote about it in different ways. Most of the time, it was the sound of the bullet hitting its mark. Even that took years to where I could hear that distinct, yet subtle, but undeniable sound of a bullet hitting its mark. It has always been there because after you've hunted a while, you know when you connect, even if the animal tears off running at a full gate.

As the February snows of Alaska were driving me insane, I decided I needed something big to look forward to. Memorial Day would certainly be a GREAT time in the sound. I had actually never been there in the spring, but what the hell, the snow was forcing me to think about greener days, so I made the request.

The air service I worked for had three houseboats placed at precarious coves around the eastern side of Prince William Sound. I asked to go out for an early season weekend and the permission was granted.

As I arrived in the Valdez office on Friday afternoon, Roger asked me which houseboat I preferred. I told him Bear Trap Bay, just in case I saw a black fuzzy thing that needed to be shot. So with that I made the quick drive to the airport and the Cessna 206 on amphibs waiting for me. Amphibs are floats with wheels in case you need to land on the ground. They land on the water just like any other floatplane, but on the runway I always characterized them like a shopping cart going too fast.

We loaded up the plane and took off. The wind was gusting over the glaciers so we flew the "long way" around and skirted the native village of Tatitlik. A 30-minute flight later and we were landing at Bear Trap Bay. I had taken my kids to this very cove four years ago, but this time there were no children. Only me and one well-equipped houseboat stood against the Alaska wilderness. Well, it was *close* to being well equipped, as I would find out later.

It was early in the season and houseboats had recently been put in place, launched from their winter dry-dock in Cordova. They were driven out by a pilot and a guide, and followed by another in a 22-foot Boston Whaler. Together, they set the anchor, did some pre-season de-winterizing and got them into semi-ready form. Memorial Day weekend was in the middle of this process.

All the houseboats were not even near the point where we sent out the cleaning crew to spruce them up for clients. In part these would be some of my duties while I was out in the great outdoors.

I sat around the houseboat for the first couple of hours getting my bearings. Then I decided to fire up one of the 10-foot skiffs assigned to each houseboat, picked up the fishing rod, my 30.06 and went looking for adventure.

The tide was high and opened up the head of the bay for boat travel, so I turned into the little cove just before the head of the bay. I say little but it was probably 300 yards long by 75 yards wide and fairly deep once you crossed the opening, which went dry during lower tides.

I saw a black bear rummaging the beach and sat and looked at him for a while. He got nervous and ran into the trees. I motored over to where he had entered the forest and got out to look for him. The light was already low in the sky so I didn't look very long before returning to my skiff and heading back to the comforts of the houseboat.

By the time I got back the sun had set behind the mountains but there was still a bit of ambient light to sit on the dock of the boat and watch Prince William Sound turn from day to the dark of night.

I had the start of a headache; I had forgotten to have my morning coffee and this is usually the outcome, so I checked the first aid kit. It had one packet of two Advil. I opened it and took them. My "going to the outdoors" kit almost always contained a small quantity of Ibuprofen and a few Imodium; I had forgotten both, as it was still early in the season. Thank God for the first aid kit.

I awoke relatively late the next day, still no coffee. The sun was already up high in the sky. It must have been around 9:30 or 10 a.m. I wasn't in any hurry to do much of anything, so I took my time making breakfast and just plain diddling around the houseboat.

It is stunningly beautiful and rustic in the Sound. Especially that time of year because the salmon runs weren't hitting yet and the normal buzz of activity during the commercial salmon season sometimes made the parts of the sound seem more like downtown Cincinnati.

Around one in the afternoon I decided to go back to the cove in which I saw the bear the night before. I took a fishing rod to catch some lunch and was kind of hoping to see the black bear again. This time I would take him. I threw in my Remington 7400 semi-automatic 30.06 rifle and strapped on my Ruger Red Hawk .44 Magnum on my shoulder harness.

Bears in the sound in the spring have the lushest and thickest coats you have ever seen. The bear I saw last night was coal black and you could tell it was thick, even from a distance.

The sun was bright and it was nearly 70 degrees already as I left the houseboat. I turned into the bay, but saw no bear. It didn't bug me too much. I knew the chances were slim, so I decided to pull on to the beach on the left of the bay and try my luck at fishing.

I thought a flounder or two would make for a fairly nice late lunch so I tied on a simple

silver spoon with a blue plastic inlay and began to cast.

On the first retrieve I saw a pollock chasing my lure. Pollock are the white fish from which imitation crabmeat is made, "it should make a nice lunch too", I thought. I changed the direction of the lure and he hit. Bam! It was a two or three pound pollock on the first cast. I caught three more in almost as many casts and decided to lie down on the beach and soak up some of the sun for a little while. It had been a long and cold winter.

I must have dozed off for a while because I did wake up. My four fish were still swimming on the stringer but the tide had gone down a few feet. It was still sunny and warm though. That's not a real common day anytime in Southcentral Alaska, so I was really enjoying it.

As I stood up, I noticed a saddle in the small hillside behind me. That is to say that the line of trees stopped and there was only a gravel rise about fifteen feet high between me and the head of the Bear Trap Bay. I walked over the top of the saddle, and a couple steps down the other side.

There, in front of me, was the expanse of the headlands to the bay. To my left braids of little streams winding their way thorough the massive stretch of now semi-dry lands which were, only hours ago, covered by seawater. It seemed to be about six football fields across and countless football fields long (I still judge distance outdoors by my high school football days).

On all sides the green mountains shot straight up. No foothills, no rolling hills, just flat then steep slope.

As I looked northwest I saw a black bear across the bay and a bit to the left at some 900 yards. He was eating the tide leftovers and seemed to be foraging toward the water at my right.

I quickly ran to my boat, grabbed my rifle and returned. I looked over the situation, glassed the bear with my binoculars and planned out my stalk.

I rarely shoot over 100 yards, not because I am a bad shot, just because I think the stalk is my favorite part of a hunt.

The first 200 yards was the easy part. I traveled northwest behind the cover of trees that lined the flats. When I was directly across from him, I waited until he was pointing in the opposite direction and I eased myself down onto the flats. We were now on even ground but still 700 yards separated us.

Between the bear and me were a few tufts of newly grown grasses, a couple shallow streambeds and lots of sunshine. The latter not the best for providing cover, especially since I was wearing old faded Carhartt pants and a white T-shirt - not the best camouflage I could have planned.

He was looking away when I started across the flats so I could walk semi-quickly or at least as quickly as I could hunkered down while keeping my knees bent. I made it a hundred and fifty yards or so relatively quickly. Then he began to turn toward me.

I laid flat in hopes the six-inch grasses would hide me well enough. When he finally began eating and facing the mountains again, I was up only as far as I had to be to move. This time I made it 40 or 50 yards before he turned again.

There were times I had to stay in the extremely uncomfortable crouching position for 10 or more minutes at a time. I know it doesn't sound like a long time when you are reading this, but my legs would really hurt until I got permission, by his turning his head away again, to move.

This game of freeze and run lasted for another 45 minutes before I covered the full 600 yards to get within shooting distance. Sometimes I'd make only a few yards, others quite a few. Sometimes I'd hide behind small tufts of grass, sometimes I just had to crouch in a shallow gully.

When I was a kid in Montana, my friends and I had a 'macho' contest and we would do these kinds of stalks and carry only one bullet. We were a bit young and arrogant but one of us would always hold up our one bullet and say something to the effect of "cause I won't need a second." We came back game-less most of the time.

I finally got to where I estimated my distance at a hundred yards; I laid on my stomach and set the sights. I placed the shot right behind the front quarter as the bruin was facing toward my right. It was a broadside shot. I squeezed the trigger and the rifle let out a bang.

The bear took off in the direction it was already facing but I knew I had missed. I can only speculate how I knew, but still I knew. He ran closer to the trees when I squeezed the trigger the second time.

This time, there was no sound, no completion. I had a malfunction. The bear slowed to a walk but he was still moving to try and escape. He must not have been sure where I was because he wasn't hurrying.

I took out the magazine and attempted a dry fire. The semi-auto action wasn't engaging fully forward when I cocked it. I removed the shell from the chamber, cycled the action again

all while keeping an eye on the bear that was still not bolting.

If this had been a brown bear chances are I would be dealing with an entirely different scenario. A brownie would likely charge. It's a little behavior they have which is not unreminicent of a schoolyard bully. Why not? They have the size to do so. They will charge at a threat before they even know what something is. Black bears are usually a bit different. I was thankful it was a black bear at the moment, even though I had my hog-leg .44 Magnum as a backup.

When I cycled the action again it hung up a quarter inch from fully closing, I applied a little pressure and it closed the rest of the way with a solid thud. It sounded complete. I pulled the trigger and heard the click of the firing pin. It, too, sounded complete. I replaced the magazine and cycled the action.

When I looked up, the bear had walked up on some large boulders that were next to the tidal flat right at the tree line. He was broadside and standing still. I placed the front sight right behind his shoulder, lifted the rear sight to cradle the front, checked the aim against the vital area and squeezed the trigger. Boom! The rifle fired. The noise, which ever so slightly filled my ears, was the sound of completion. I knew it hit.

I didn't wait; I stood directly up and began walking toward the bear. I couldn't see it as it had disappeared into the trees but there was no doubt in my mind it was hit, and hit solidly.

As I walked closer to the trees, I laid down my rifle against a big rock and pulled my Red Hawk from its sheath. I could hear the bear moaning and groaning somewhere back up in the trees, but not too far.

As I picked my way carefully through the thick black spruce stand, guided always by the bear's noises, I pulled back the hammer on the pistol. It was packing a 300-grain load I bought at the local sporting goods store just for bears. When I saw him, it would be close quarters.

The moaning seemed to be coming from the north and the way the rocks and the trees were positioned, I couldn't get a view of the bear before I was closer than I liked. I decided to loop over the top of the locale and see if the other side would provide a better approach. It was only about 30 feet up from the beach, so I climbed higher and moved in with the bear to my south. I could see an opening in the cover which would afford me a sight on the bear from 25 feet, much farther than I would have from the other direction.

As I peered in to the small clearing, I saw movement. It was something black and seemed

rather small. As I looked terrible thoughts crossed my mind. I wondered if I had missed the bear and accidentally hit an unseen cub. It certainly seemed small enough.

Then, what appeared to be an armature protruded from the small black form and lifted itself towards the sky. I had no idea what I was looking at. I was flabbergasted.

The armature then curved downwardly and when it reached the ground, its true identity took shape. I was looking at a bear's ass and the armature now looked like a back leg positioning itself to push its owner's body out of the hole in which it had fallen.

I took a few steps to position my self closer and pointed the barrel at the torso.

As the bear began to pull the front of its body out of the hole, my thought was that I was lucky and it was going to free itself, then I could pull the trigger and end the hunt with the bear not in a hole, therefore saving me the work of pulling him out.

Thank God reason set in before it was too late. The realization hit me that if this wounded bear freed itself from the hole and saw me, the half a second I would have to make the shot wouldn't seem like near long enough.

He pulled most of his torso up out of the

hole, enough to expose his vitals. I chose, quite wisely I might add, to squeeze the trigger and dispatch the beast before he could see me. It worked. He collapsed back into the hole, limp. Completion.

Then the arduous task of getting him out began. He weighed around 300 pounds or so and nearly all of him was in a hole not much bigger than he was. I pulled on a hind leg. I pulled on the other hind leg. I pulled on both hind legs. Finally, I got him up and rolled him out of the hole.

When I first shot him, I had it in my mind to get a half body mount. I thought it would be a nice addition to the rugs I already had. Plus he had a perfect white "v" on his chest. But during the removal from the hole, it was obvious that this was the thickest coat I had ever seen or felt on a bear. Therefore, he would have to become a rug for the wall.

I hadn't noticed, but during the struggle to remove him from his cave, I was developing a huge headache. I am not one to get migraines, but this was the most excruciating headache I had ever had. Again, no morning coffee.

I rolled him down off the rock nearer the tidal flats and sat down to catch my breath. I was not looking forward to carrying him, either

in parts or whole the nearly 1000 yards to my boat.

As I sat wondering, "What did I do to myself?" I noticed that the high tide marks were very near where I was standing. I took a mental note, the tide was still at its low point. Then one of those "Hey! Great ideas!" hit me. If I just waited a few hours, the tide would be right near where I was sitting and I may have to move him 20 feet or so instead of thousands of feet. This seemed like the plan. Plus my headache was already throbbing, so I figured I'd take a nap and come back later when I can drive right up to this spot.

I tied some florescent orange surveyor's tape around a rock so I would find it again with little effort and left.

By the time I walked back to the skiff and drove it back to the houseboat my headache was undeniable. I went to the medicine chest, but no luck. I had taken the only pain relievers last night. I was out.

I knew I wouldn't sleep with my head in that much pain so I had to think. I knew there was another houseboat a few miles away in Comfort Cove, but I didn't know if it had any pain pills in its first aid kit. Still, I had to try. I jumped into the skiff, took an extra container of gas and took off in the direction of my target. Having never been to this particular cove before, I only knew where it was from seeing it from the air on the way in. It was a lot further on the water than it was flying in a plane. It took 20 minutes to finally turn into the mouth of the cove.

The houseboat was locked, but I found a way in through a window. Luckily there were two packets containing two Advil each. I hoped it was enough. I took two, put the other packet in my pocket, and drove back.

I woke up with no headache, so that was promising. Shortly afterwards, I realized I had a bear to deal with and prayed the tide was high enough to enable me to drive close to it. When I arrived at the head of the bay, it was like a place I had never been before. A large expanse of water lay before me and far, far over to the side, right next to the waterline was orange tape strung around a rock. My tape, my rock, my bear.

The tide played better than I could have expected. The bear was about five feet from the water. I pulled almost right up to it and rolled it in my boat whole. This was much better than having to carry it, even in parts for nearly a mile. Nice!

I drove the skiff back to the houseboat. It had an Astroturf-covered floating dock attached with the leading edge near water level so you

could literally drive right up onto the dock and step out on dry dock. This meant you could also skin and quarter a bear carcass in a relatively clean environment, free of dirt and rocks. What an unexpected treat.

Within an hour I had it skinned, quartered, and bagged. There was a minor incident with the remaining carcass not wanting to sink, it was quickly solved by taking the skiff to shore and getting a substantial rock to tie on as weight, but the rest of the trip was just another beautiful weekend in Prince William Sound.

The pilot landed to pick me up around noon the next day. When he landed, he said he had a headache and walked towards the first aid kit. Unfortunately for him, my head felt fine.

The houseboat in Bear Trap Bay

The Upper Kenai, where big lies are created

More, Bigger, Better Than You

I was getting convinced, as the two of us drove down the Seward Highway headed for fishing, that Chris was a compulsive liar. Of course we are talking about fishermen but this is the kind of lying where all the other liars, standing around in a liars group, hear him and say, "Damn! Now that's a liar!" He had already told me that he sang with the well known rock groups REM and the B-52s. He told me that "network" talent scouts sent him to Alaska to groom him for *"The anchor job."* I'll never forget the way he so dramatically turned his head my direction and with a totally straight face queried, "I don't have to tell you what THEE anchor job is, do I?"

Chris was a late edition anchor on a local TV station, a network affiliate. He had some talent but I didn't see "network anchor" talent and last I heard, Alaska was not the hot bed farm club for the network jobs. But I wasn't in the circles of network talent scouts, so I couldn't say for sure.

I knew he wanted to catch fish, that's why he was with me, and silvers and rainbows were why we were driving south to the Kenai Peninsula that early September morning.

He asked me to take him, not because he didn't know how to fish -- he proclaimed that he was very good... even an expert large mouth bass angler. I guess he didn't hear me when I told him I used to fish bass tournaments in Oregon and Ohio because he kept saying "You salmon fishermen are different!"

Sunrise is around 7:30 a.m. that time of year at that latitude, so we left at 5:30 a.m. We got to the parking lot after literally dozens of totally unbelievable yarns spun by Chris, near one of my favorite secret Kenai rainbow holes at seven and geared up for the walk in, which takes around 20 minutes. I had on a coat, polarized sunglasses I used to sight cast, and hip waders. Chris had a brand new, and his first ever I might add, pair of neoprene chest waders, and a big blue down-filled coat, both of which play prominently later in this story. He asked me why I wasn't wearing chest waders. I told him, "They get me into places I probably shouldn't be in."

On the Sterling Highway the parking lot is exactly one and a half miles from the "Entering Game Management Unit 14B" sign. You have to turn across the oncoming traffic lane to find parking. After a short walk by a back slough, you follow the river's cut bank for a third of a mile and cross a couple gravel bars. That's where most people stop. We went further, which is why I call this a "secret hole." It's further than most will walk and it's not convenient for floaters to stop here, so even they pass it by.

After the gravel bars the trail to the hole goes through some woods and breaks out at a side channel. Cross that and it's the island off which I call the secret rainbow hole. As we arrived he reiterated, "You salmon fishermen are strange. We never have to walk this far for bass!"

He even picked on the daily bag limits of salmon and trout. "For bass", he told me, "you can keep ten a day, what's this three for salmon and one for rainbow? I wouldn't even have gone as often as I did if I could have only kept three!"

We tied on terminal tackle upon arrival at the hole. I taught him to tie a simple improved clinch knot and gave him an egg-sucking-leech for a fly. I tied on an egg pattern. It was really a bare gamagatsu hook with a foam egg imitation slid over the point to the shank of the hook. Both set-ups had a two-foot leader, then a swivel with an egg sinker free sliding above.

Chris hooked the first bow; it was a nice one I guessed to be around 24 inches. Chris fought it for a few minutes. It jumped a few times and his rod went limp, which is why I had to guess at the size. He tried to blame the hook as being too dull. I was convinced that something else was dull but I didn't think it was the hook. "You trout fishermen!" he said.

The guide in me takes over when I am fishing with inexperienced anglers. This was no different, so when he had hooked up, I reeled in, grabbed a net and began coaching. After he lost the fish I had to grab my rod and start over. I hooked up next. The rainbow jumped which alerted me that I had one on.

This was rainbow fishing in the 'big water' of the main channel, which moved fast and was deep. It caused the arc in the line to be substantial enough to hide a lot of strikes, but I developed a theory that big rainbows, among other places, find still water below the current and sit in those holes picking off food as it drifts over head. These are the fish I was targeting at the moment. It also made for a lot fewer snags for the lesser-experienced fishermen, or in this case, bass fisherman.

I fought the fish for a little while, got him tired enough that I could net him with my left hand while controlling his head with my right. I posed for a picture that Chris took with his yellow disposable camera. It was a buck. I could tell by the shape of its head and the groove in the tip of his upper lip. I placed a tape to him as he lay, 23 inches. Chris asked if I was going to keep it. I said, "No. I never keep rainbows. Anyway the size limit was 24 inches or better." I revived him for a few seconds while holding his tail, then he bolted into the current.

We fished and caught and released for a few hours on the big water, but as the light got higher in the sky, I left Chris and the big water and turned my attention toward the small channel behind the island. I had been working on using an old bass technique for these rainbows during the middle of the day.

During my largemouth obsession days, I used to employ "vertical jigging" in fallen timbers. This was the art of casting a line over a branch or a fallen tree and using that as a fulcrum off which one could jig up and down for the big largemouth.

It should work here, too, because when the light got bright, the rainbows sometimes went to the timbers for cover. There they would lie and wait to ambush prey which would unknowingly swim or drift by. The only trick was to have strong enough leader to horse them out of the timber and into the open water once they jumped to free the hook. If you didn't get them out of the timbers when they first jumped, the line... well you know what monofilament line does around timbers.

I caught a couple nice bows this way off the mainland side of the braid in some branches of a couple fallen trees and decided to wade back across to check on Chris. I looked left about mid-stream and noticed some branches sticking up out of the water near the head of the island. I decided to investigate.

I found a couple of trees lying underneath the water parallel to the shore. With my polarized glasses I could see the rounded silhouette of a fish's head between the two tree trunks. The blackness of the head informed me this was a rainbow. They truly look black from above, where the Dollies look grayer and the salmon look more dull silver, or dark red, depending on their time in the fresh water.

I cast upstream from the predator and let my egg pattern drift into his head. It bounced off and he spooked. I started to stand upright to continue over to Chris when in the corner of my vision, I saw the black round head return. I squatted behind the bush behind which I had been hiding and cast upstream again. I watched the egg drift just right a second time, but when it was right in front of the fish, I noticed this head was a lot bigger than it was before. It was about twice as big.

The egg slipped into the fish's mouth and just as I was about to set the hook, I saw him spit it forward but he didn't spook. My heart dropped to the muddy bank. I took a gamble that he may take it a second time if I presented it just right, so I did a roll cast up stream again, and again presented the perfect drift. He took it again and just as fast, spit it out again. I was amazed. Again, he didn't spook. There would be no way in the world he would take it a third time, but since he was still there, I cast a third time.

When the egg reached his snout, he wouldn't budge. He didn't take it, he didn't spook and he wouldn't budge. A really big rainbow is so big you can see his gill plates moving from a few feet away. I could see this one breathing. My egg held in place by my taut line, right in front of his mouth. He moved up, just for a second, and mouthed the egg. I missed another chance to set the hook but I left the egg in the same place. Hoping, praying, and mentally begging for him to mouth it one more time.

It was the slightest flick of his tail which made me pull the fly line in my hand and when I did, my right arm lifted the rod up. There was resistance and a huge splash followed as the rainbow shot like a rocket out of the water shaking and spitting to try and free himself from the sting in his mouth. The tugs at my arm were surprisingly heavy and violently strong.

When he hit the open current, he swam fast and hard. My Lamiglas rod bent like a willow in a hurricane. I jammed the fighting butt into my groin and pulled back on the cork handle while my Cortland reel's drag buzzed. He was taking out line and heading down stream. When the line shot across the water directly away from me, I knew he was going to jump so I dropped my tip and "bowed to my partner" as the saying among fly-fishermen goes.

I am always amazed at how the big fish flops compared to the smaller fish that just seems to shake as he jumps. Maybe I am not describing it correctly because it's not less impressive. It looks slower but so much more powerful. I guess I compare it to the difference in the power in the deep rumble of a big Harley Davidson V-Twin 88 cubic inch engine to the faster, yet whinier, buzz of a Yamaha 4 cylinder 500 cc engine. You feel the Harley, you hear the Yamaha. This rainbow was the Harley compared to the Yamahas we had been catching.

He jumped and ran a few more times, but I finally got him tired enough to "tail" him. I took him out of the water and ran across the island to where Chris was still casting out into the big water. He started to say: "Where have you been?" but the last part of that just kind of faded out when he saw what was in my hands.

"Is that a rainbow?" he asked. "That's a huge rainbow!" I said, "Take my picture with him before I let him go." He quickly reeled in and pulled the camera from his jacket. I dropped to one knee and made him take a couple quick shots. I then laid the fish in a shallow bit of water and pulled my tape out. I drew it across the fish from head to tail. Thirty two inches right at the tip of the tail. I re-checked my right hand to make sure I hadn't moved it from the tip of the nose, looked back at the tape in my left hand and got thirty two inches again. "Damn! That's a nice fish!" I said, "It's my biggest rainbow ever."

Chris began to tell me a story of his biggest large mouth bass, which just happened to be over 32 inches, but I stopped him short by interrupting him and asking him to go put my rod up against a tree. I really had no reason for my rod to go up against the tree but it did stop his "better than you" story. Plus I didn't have the heart to tell him that the world record largemouth was around 32 inches. His was obviously "bigger."

Now I have caught bigger steelhead but they run to the ocean, this was a resident rainbow of the upper Kenai. Chris asked if I was going to keep it. I repeated, "I don't keep rainbows." He said, "Yeah but this is a huge rainbow, you could keep just this one." I remember thinking, "Why couldn't I? I never keep rainbows, I could keep this one." But then I remembered that I release them for future fisherman, either to be caught again or to breed. I should release him. But this wasn't a hen that could lay thousands of eggs, it was a buck! I could keep this one, couldn't I. Chris said, "If this was a largemouth bass, I'd keep it."

By the time I finally quit debating the idea, I looked at the fish, he was still lying on his side and only about a quarter of him was in the water, the rest was exposed to the air. I thought, "He's been out of the water too long to release now. He'd just swim off and die." I took the fish bonker and smacked him hard on the head. He did the steely-eyed quiver of death. The decision was made and the sentence was carried out.

I felt both remorse and glee about my decision. Chris was just excited. He wanted to pose with the fish so he could send pictures to his dad back in Georgia who was supposed to be the guy who taught Chris his expertise in large mouth bass. He posed, I snapped. We fished the hole another hour or so and left to go to the car and have lunch.

Normally this would be the climax to my tale but this story really isn't about the rainbow as much as it is about fishing partners.

After lunch Chris still wanted to fish so I told him I knew a hole where the silvers should be in and if they are they should be thick this time of year. He was agreeable, so we drove back toward Anchorage. At the junction where the road to Hope, Alaska meets the Seward Highway, I told him to take the turn. We weren't going all the way to the town, but I knew of a spot right down from the highway.

Taking the first pullout with a guard rail on the north side of the road, the path leads almost directly down from the road to Six Mile Creek. It's a clear running stream that also doubles for gold panners and white water rafters as a destination. Usually only locals come here to fish.

Where the path runs into the bank stands a wall eight feet above the water with no beach on which to stand, but there is a fairly good hole as the water comes from a shallow rapids into a deeper hole. We saw some silvers as we arrived at the trees. I thought we would save those for later in case we didn't find any in the pool above the rapids.

The pool was almost a perfect circle right below some big class three or four white water, depending on the time of year, squeezing down to a thin chute between high cliff walls of solid rock. I am sure the rafters are relieved when they hit the calm waters of the pool after the treacherous run they just went through in the canyon that leads here.

The western edge of the pool is more shallow and transitions into the rapids, only about two feet deep, as the water picks up speed. It was in the pool we saw the bigger school of silvers. We fished for a while from the south bank of the pool; Chris caught one nice silver at about eight pounds and stuck it on a stringer.

The school of fish had adjusted to our presence at the shore, so we decide to try to cross so as to cast from the other side and get a better presentation.

Chris, with his chest waders, led the way. About half way I took a little wave over the top of my hip waders and told Chris I was not going to be able to make it. He crossed anyway, focusing on the silvers we saw from the other bank. I left and waded back to shore.

As I watched, Chris cast the water into a froth. I went back to the higher bank of the first hole to try my luck at the few silvers we had seen on the original decent from the highway. I stood casting above the fish and letting my fly drift down toward them.

By the time I had made my third cast, Chris was obviously giving up on his quarry in the pool because I saw him beginning his traverse of the tailing of the pool. I was watching out of the corner of my eye when his trouble began.

He was attempting his cross in shallower water where the current was stronger than his original cross. He stumbled once and recovered fine. It was after the second stumble that he seemed to have lost his confidence. His legs were more wobbly and he was less sure of his footing. The third stumble was tragic for him. He grasped for a foothold and couldn't quite get a solid one. He never realized it, but his stumbles had progressively moved him down stream further and further into stronger and stronger current.

When he went down for the final time it was on his back. His feet were leading as he drifted into the rapids. He began to scream my name in sheer terror. 'Rick! Rick!" he yelled. I thought about helping him but there was little I could do and he really wasn't in that much trouble. The water was only a couple of feet deep and getting shallower as he drifted.

"Rick! Rick!" he screamed again as he drifted with the current. It truly fit the old description of 'screaming bloody murder.' His chest waders had obviously filled with water, which was helping him along downstream with the current. If he had on hip waders, he could have kicked them off, not with chest waders.

I was having a difficult time not showing the convulsions of the laughter which had overtaken me, but I pretended that I was unaware of his plight. It was double hard to control when I saw his small tackle box go floating by my position.

He was almost like a big blue bird trying to fly backward as the now drenched arms of his down coat where flailing to keep him afloat on his back. The water was flying from his arms with every flail spraying in vertical sheets, as he continued to scream for me to help him. Down jackets can really keep you warm in the cold when they are dry, I guess I never realized how much water they soaked up when wet, until now.

He finally gave up on trying to right himself from the backwards position, and gave up on screaming for me, and lunged forward onto his stomach. He began to try and swim his way free of his torment.

With my eyes down I saw his disposable camera float past me, then the butt of his rod. The camera contained the pictures of my big rainbow but I thought I could find it later, down stream.

Unfortunately for Chris the water was only about 15 or 18 inches deep at that point in the rapids and he was bloodying his knuckles with each stroke in his attempt to swim. He tried stroke after stroke but couldn't get the gravel to let go, as I am sure his knees were dragging. I was having a very difficult time concealing my laughter watching out of the corner of my eye while keeping my head forward. It was the hardest thing not to turn and look right.

The show only lasted a couple of minutes in total, but by the time I was about to pee on myself, Chris made a radical choice. He stood up. It worked. The water was only three quarters of the way up to his knee. I kept my head directly forward as I watched him slosh out onto the bank.

After ten minutes I thought I could convincingly pull off that I had not been witness to his near drowning. I went to find him. He wasn't difficult to track; I just had to follow the water trail. When I finally caught up to him, he was just crawling over the guardrail, still drenched, carrying his silver.

I said, "Hey Chris, you look a little wet." When he turned, he said, "I will never let you convince me to cross a river that I have never crossed before!" He was angry, and it seemed to be at me! I chuckled. His comment didn't really make any sense, but I didn't figure pointing out the total lack of logic would gain me any favors. Plus it was still a two-hour drive home.

He bitched a little about losing everything down the river so that gave me ample excuse to go and look, at least for the camera. After all, it contained the only pictures of my rainbow while alive. I went alone, as he was feeling too wet to climb up and down the bank. I searched for 20 minutes or so but finally gave up and walked back to the car. He wasn't any less angry yet.

He cooled down over the course of the quick drive home. Probably not for him as he was really wet, but it went fast for me. When he dropped me off, he wanted to have me take a picture of his one silver. We stood outside the garage and snapped a picture since all the other pictures went floating down Six Mile Creek. After the picture, he had to use the bathroom so we went inside.

When he stepped inside, he saw my fish and game mounts on the walls. He looked at the king salmon, "Wow, how big was that?" He saw the halibut tail, "Is that a whales tail?" which was understandable for a Lower 48er. Then he looked across the living room towards the hall. There was a greenish fish I had caught in Ohio. He walked up to look directly at it and said, "Wow, what do you call that kind of fish?" I replied, "I don't know what you bass fisherman from Georgia call them, but everywhere I ever lived, we called those largemouth bass." It was about a six-pound largemouth I had caught years before.

I guess I have always been kind of glad his disposable camera was lost down the river. Not that I don't wish I had the pictures of my biggest rainbow, but I am really glad I never had to hear the story later from someone we both knew in common, saying "Did you ever see the picture of Chris's 32-inch rainbow he caught on the upper Kenai?"

My buddy Dave and one out of thousands

While You Still Can

There have been too many events in life that have been put off, then never realized. When I lived in Cleveland, Ohio I always intended to go visit the Football Hall of Fame in Canton. It was only 30 miles away, but I could always wait until next weekend. I never made it.

I was always planning to go visit my grandfather for a week's vacation. He's no longer with us.

There are outdoors opportunities that come our way once, only to be lost forever.

This is a story about one of those "it could start snowing at any second" days. The cold bite of winter was not just around the corner, it was here and its teeth were already into my flesh. Late

September in Naknek, a small fishing community on the shores of Bristol Bay, could be in the 60's or it could be in the low 30's like it was today. It could actually be colder, but the drama of the story precluded me from going there.

This day included me, Dave Taylor and Sonny Groat, all three co-workers at the construction firm and the largest herd of caribou I have ever seen. Dave and I were imports from the big city of Anchorage; Sonny was born and raised on the shores of Bristol Bay. That's why we agreed it was best for him to drive the skiff. Well, that and it was his skiff!

We left the city dock at king salmon, 15 miles east of Naknek traveling down stream on the Naknek River, heading for Smelt Creek. It was named, obviously, for the large run of smelt that head up the creek every year to spawn. That was not this time of year, but the creek still carried the name.

Sonny's skiff is standard faire for bush Alaska, a 16-foot Lund aluminum skiff with three bench seats and a 35 horse outboard with an extended tiller handle drive. The driver stood next to the outboard, usually straddling one of the portable gas tanks while the passengers sit on a bench seat facing forward. That was the arrangement this day, too.

Sonny told us we would find caribou up the creek so we planned this hunt come rain or shine. It was cold and cloudy at 2 p.m. when we hit the confluence of Smelt Creek and the Naknek River. The day was going to get no warmer or brighter. Folks who spend their lives on select waterways know them like the back of their own hands, and Sonny knew this creek. It was evident the way he knew where each rock garden was a turn or two before we got there, and he would call them out to us before we hit them. For the most shallow runs he would get speed built up and tilt the motor at the last second as we could hear the scraping of the hull against the gravel.

The creek was windy and as we traveled further and further upstream the flatlands became rolling hills next to the creek. We saw a few red fox as we traveled, but no caribou until after the first 45 minutes. Then as we rounded the bend, there they were: five caribou. I reached for my gun, but Sonny said to wait. "They aren't big enough and they are already too far off the creek to shoot."

After you hunt in rural Alaska long enough, you begin to see the wisdom of the locals not bothering to shoot the animals more than a few yards from the water. It's because you have to pack them that far and there will always be one near the water if you wait. Sonny urged us to wait. Every time we saw a small herd, they were bolting away from the creek and Sonny said "Naw! Wait."

It was raining slightly and the wind caused by the movement of the boat made it even colder than it already was, so Dave pulled out one of the hazmat coveralls we had for work and slipped into it to stay dry. It looked kind of funny because it was head-to-toe yellow.

By 4 p.m. Dave was getting worried that we were getting too far-gone and we wouldn't have enough fuel to return. He began to ask Sonny to turn around. Sonny just smiled that easy smile he had and said, "Wait, you're going to love this." Although he never clarified what "this" was.

By 4:30 p.m. Dave was pressuring Sonny fairly hard to turn around when the creek opened up and we were all of a sudden on Smelt Lake. It was a fairly large lake, just kind of plopping onto the tundra for no apparent reason, but there it was, and there we were. Sonny drove straight out into the middle and just kept on going. Once we got near the far side he pointed to the shore and said "What about that?" I looked. It was a herd of about 30 or 40 caribou, right near the lake's waterline with a couple really nice bulls mixed in with the herd. Sonny said he would drive straight at them, but they would run when we got real close, so be ready to jump off as the bow hit the shore and shoot the bull you want. Dave and I agreed.

The caribou ran a bit earlier than Sonny wanted, but we didn't stray from the plan. As the bow slid up on the tundra I leapt and ran after the bou. They were over the hill before I had a shot, so I ran to the top, thinking they may stop right on the other side like mule deer back home.

There are a set of rules for hunting caribou; number three is "you can't run down a walking caribou." It's a fact, and these weren't walking. By the time I reached the top of the hill they were already three hilltops away from me. I couldn't even tell the bull with my scope. I lay down to catch my breath.

It was nice to feel the cool breeze run across my face. The smell of the tundra is almost pungent, in a good way, in the fall. It smells like "the hunt." Lying on tundra is similar to laying on an air mattress, a crunchy air mattress, but an air mattress nonetheless. I lay there nearly five minutes before the other two caught up to me and gave me a start by speaking. I sat up to answer and we began a light conversation about chasing a critter that can run three times faster than humans on flat ground. As we talked I was gazing across the lake to the eastern shore when the entire hillside seemed to shift diagonally. "I must be so winded I am dizzy," I thought.

The shift happened again, but this time I was more aware. It was the entire hillside moving all right but it wasn't tundra, it was 5,000 or so caribou. The herd was massive, and I had never seen such a sight before. I couldn't make out which were bulls and which were cows, but I could see the forest of caribou. I pointed to them and muttered something I am sure was unintelligible. It was enough so they both turned to look though. "Oh my God," they said, almost in unison.

The wind was blowing from our backs but looking at the wave patterns on the lake, it wasn't blowing directly to them. It was quartering to the right. We surmised that we could motor to the left and set up a drift to the shore directly below them without them scenting us and spooking. To the boat we walked, me with clumps of tundra hanging off my back.

The boat worked exactly as we planned. We motored to the left, then drifted to the right and came to rest below a small rise directly below the herd. Quietly we climbed out of the skiff, walked up the hill then crawled to the crest. Before we peered over the top, we agreed to pick our prospective bulls, count to three and fire. I, with my Winchester Model 70 .338 magnum and Dave with a 7mm mag he had borrowed from Sonny, peered over the top. Starting at about 75 yards and extending to 400 yards was a gigantic herd of over 5,000 caribou just grazing away.

We were south of the Naknek River, so these were biologically classified as the Aleutian herd. Most of the caribou I had hunted to that point were Mulchatna caribou. These looked different. They seemed heavier in the body but shorter and stockier. They were also lighter in color. Many claim that 50 years ago when reindeer were being professionally herded in Alaska by an influx of Laplanders, the reindeer escaped and crossed with the indigenous populations of Alaska caribou. The not so accepted in public forums, yet almost universally accepted in private conversations, is that there are no pure indigenous caribou left anywhere in the state, they have all been mixed with formerly domestic stocks of reindeer. I am of the later school of thought.

I placed my scope on what looked to be a good-sized rack. It was a bull that would definitely range in the books of Boone and Crockett. The beams were massive; they almost looked like they were bending under their own weight. I know that doesn't happen but it certainly looked that way. He was inside the herd a ways - I guessed around 125 yards.

I whispered to Dave that I had my bull, he asked which one. When I finally got him to see it, he agreed it was huge. I said "Pick your bull." I waited a few seconds and repeated, "Pick your bull." He said, "I can't find one that big." I tersely responded, "There probably isn't another one that big. Pick your damn bull."

The herd began to move, I think because Sonny stood full erect to see what the herd contained. He didn't care. This was just another day that he could or could not bring home game. He lived here and this was his backyard. We were like five-year-olds on Christmas morning.

Dave said again, "I can't find one as big as yours."

I replied, "Just pick one close."

He mumbled something incoherent, but at the end I caught, "I'm just not finding one."

I broke the visual lock I had on the record books and scanned the bulls to my right, where he was supposed to be looking. I found a decent bull and pointed him out.

Dave said, "My scope is fogged up."

I replied "For Christ's sake! I've lost over 100 yards on this bull"

He said, " Ok, sh.."

He didn't have to finish, I pulled the trigger. Click.

It seemed to be a loud click, but it was no boom. There was no smoke, no smell of burning gunpowder, no muzzle flash. Just a "click".

The click echoed, but I am sure it was in my head. All I know is that when you are expecting a boom and all you hear is a click, it's the loudest click in the world.

I looked at my rifle, then at Dave, then back at my rifle, then at the bull still moving away. Then I looked back at Dave and pulled the .338 back from my shoulder, butt down towards my hip. The barrel was pointing diagonally in the air at about 40 degrees up when the boom finally came. Boom.

I was taken aback. I looked up at Dave, he looked at the just fired gun, still smoking, then at me and said "You've got a problem." Like the unexpected click, the boom when you're not expecting a boom is the loudest boom you'll ever hear.

I looked to the herd of caribou, they were moving at a substantial clip away from us. I fiddled with the bolt action until I figured out how to make it fire. Unfortunately, after the firing pin worked once, I had to take the bolt out and manually re-set it to fire again. The procedure I devised took 30 seconds though, so while the gun was still functional, its effectiveness was impeded greatly, thereby eroding my effectiveness.

Sonny asked if I had it working, I said "Good enough." He said they were heading down stream next to the creek, if we got to the boat we could head them off. We ran.

Sonny fired up the motor and we took off out of the lake and down the creek. We twisted and turned catching glimpses of the herd, first to the left, then to the right. While the biggest bulls seemed to be out near the front, they weren't actually twisting, they were running in a straight line. On the other hand we were twisting and turning with the meandering path of the creek.

Sonny pulled the skiff over to the left side of the creek and said they should be coming right over that hill in a few minutes. Dave and I ran to the top of the hill, saw the herd coming and spotted a willow stand that would provide great cover. Again, we ran.

By the time we got to the cover the big bulls had passed us by and all we saw were cows, calves and young bulls running in groups of 20 or 30. We hurried. Notice I didn't say we ran, back to the boat. We were getting tired. Sonny thought we could head them off again so we took off.

Down stream we went again, this time we caught the middle of the herd crossing the creek. It was a real National Geographic moment watching them come down the bank, jump in the water, and pull themselves out, like drowning rats, up the other side and pick right back up to the pace they trotted before. We had to sit for at least a hundred to cross before there was enough of a lull for us to motor through.

This time, Sonny got us way ahead of them before he pulled over. When he did, we jumped out of the boat, with a little rest we were running again and we spotted good cover from which to launch our ambush. We waited and waited, crouched down behind the brush. It seemed like quite a time that we waited when all of a sudden I noticed Sonny was almost standing right next to us.

He said the herd had turned and went a new direction a couple hundred yards before our ambush spot. He said he had watched them turn from the skiff and we might as well head back to the boat, which we did.

We slowly traveled down stream for 15 or 20 minutes when we saw a small herd of about fifteen small bulls and cows standing near the creek a few dozen yards from us. Sonny pulled over. He didn't have to say anything. Dave and I didn't have to say anything. We climbed out of the boat, shouldered our rifles, counted to three and fired. I dropped one small two-year-old bull, Dave dropped a cow. They weren't much for size, but we finally got some caribou meat for the winter.

We gutted and loaded them whole and headed down stream. The rest of the trip was relaxed except for the running out of fuel and Sonny raiding locals hunting cabins using lantern gas and cooking gas for fuel to finish the trip. He said he knew every personal cabin he raided and that he would replace the fuel for them.

We took the caribou to our home and skinned and boned them. I always planned to go back up Smelt Creek, to hunt that herd with a properly functioning weapon. I still think about the size of the herd and the sheer will to escape the color and smell of the tundra.

It will never be.

Access to land and game is fluid in Alaska. So is the management of the game. Since the 70's the State government "biologists" have been "managing" a declining resource. The predators are numerous, and the Department of Fish and Game is entrenched with bureaucrats who think their job is managing people, instead of managing the fish and the game. There are still some who are level headed, but they are so outnumbered it's not even funny.

But to put it in real perspective, I have a Native friend who has spent his entire life living off the land and researching animals in our state. He tells me that every year more game is taken in the 100 mile radius around Washington, DC than in the entire state of Alaska. That should never be the case – not in a state who's landmass is one-fifth the size of the entire Lower 48.

One example, as a result of this mismanagement, is that the caribou around Naknek and King Salmon are now off limits to me and most of the population to hunt. It's a discriminatory practice they call a Tier II hunt. Forget the legal mumbo jumbo; it means you and I can't go anymore.

Paul and the "Cub" just before the walrus

Check That Scope Before you Shoot

Hunting in Alaska is different than most places for many reasons. One big reason is that you never know what animal you may run across regardless of what you are targeting. Bears, moose, deer, wolves, goats, sheep, hare, caribou, lynx, even a cougar or a mule deer or a pheasant every now and then. But I forgot a whole other group of mammals that could show up.

Paul called, late in the afternoon, to see if I wanted to go to Montague Island for a deer hunt the next day. I usually jump at the chance to skip out of work and go hunting, so I confirmed with my boss, scheduled the day off and went home to pack.

The weather had been cold, as in single digits and less than zero, for weeks and I was sick of the cold. This being December didn't lend itself to any relief soon. I needed a change of pace. I packed warm clothes, grabbed my 30.30, slipped on my Extra Toughs (knee-high water proof boots) and drove to the strip.

Paul was already they're removing the wing covers, which were caked with frost. The cowling to the Super Cub had a quilted cover on, too. The frost on the window was the most difficult to get off. The window was plastic and the frost gripped it hard. With a plastic scraper it took quite a bit of elbow grease to get most of it clear enough for flight. Half an hour later we took off.

The Super Cub is like a backcountry Alaska 4 x 4. It's not too fast but it can take off and land in a very short distance making landing strips out of virtually any decent sand bar in a river, beach or any treeless, flat place. This 1958 beauty was equipped with a 150-horse engine, 31-inch bush tires and auxiliary fuel tanks. The wings give Cubs the lift to fly with just about any weight you can pack in or on them. Albeit not quite legal, you can often see antlers tied onto the struts under the wings during moose or caribou season.

Rising above Anchorage was rising above the flooring of an icebox, which hadn't been defrosted in years. But as we climbed the remaining frost began to melt off the window and the clouds gave way to sunshine. It's often much warmer up high than near the ground in the middle of winter in Southcentral Alaska, and today was such a day.

The flight to Montague Island took about two hours crossing the Chugach Mountains, then the many islands of Prince William Sound, until we finally skirted the coast of our destination.

Deer hunting in Alaska is unlike deer hunting elsewhere. While there is the whole half an hour before official sunrise and sunset deal, it's done often by airplane, as we were experiencing. The Alaska Department of Fish and Game even allows same-day airborne hunting of deer. This is to say, you fly around, see some deer, land, stalk the deer, shoot, load them into the plane, go look for more. It's a little more demanding than it sounds, but you get the picture.

Our first landing of the day came when we arrived at Jeanie Cove on the eastern side and the southern end of the island. There is strip we discovered a few years earlier. It used to be the beach, but during the 1964 earthquake the land rose in this particular location around 15 feet. It made for a flat, straight strip on which to land airplanes, which we did.

We had seen a couple of bucks in the tidal swamp nearby, while flying overhead and had

planned on putting the sneak on them. They were all of a mile walk down the beach, and then we would have to slosh our way into the swamp until we could get a shot. This was the plan but as often happens in Alaska, the plan has some changes along the way.

The limit of deer in that particular game management unit is five. In December that's five deer, not five bucks, not three bucks and two does. Five deer. If it's late in December, since the season only stays open until the end of the month, unless you have another trip planned, you take every deer you see. Such was the case this day.

We stepped out of the plane and the difference in temperature hit us like a ton of bricks. It must have been 35 or 40 degrees. When your body is acclimated to below zero, almost anything in the "plus" range feels great. I didn't even feel the need to take my fur hat or thick jacket. It was a nice change of pace.

As Paul was gathering his gear, I took a stroll uphill to the meadow above the strip. As I glanced across, the unmistakable outline of a deer head caught my eye and I raised the rifle. I fired, saw some movement, raised the rifle again, saw the same outline turning to leave, and fired again. Everything was quiet. I walked over and saw one deer laying in the meadow. It was the first of the twins, the second got away.

Paul showed up as I was pulling the innards out and chuckled as he said, "Does it still have milk around its mouth?" obviously joking about the small size. I laughed and told him of the second one who went up the hill. He said he would take a short walk to see if he could go and shoot it and left. I finished gutting the little thing and carried it back to the plane. Paul showed up a few minutes later and said "No, luck! He was gone."

After we took the deer back to the plane, we walked down the beach, took a guess at where the deer were in the swamp and turned in. We misjudged their location by a few hundred yards and they heard us enter the boggy terrain. Paul had a chance glimpse as the last one bolted from the area, but it wasn't enough of a glimpse to get off a shot. We missed the chance at both of them but it was still daylight for a couple more hours, so we went back to the plane.

We loaded up and headed off. Paul flew up the coast to the north a few miles as we scanned the ground for more deer, then began to climb. He wanted to check one of our favorite deer spots on the other side of the island. We crossed the center of the island where the mountains rise up

to nearly 3000 feet above sea level and descended down to the beach which is, well, sea level.

Between Hanning Bay and McCloud Harbor, on the west side of the island, there is a creek that flows in to the ocean at a dent in the near straight coastline named Fault Cove. We had taken deer here numerous times in the past. Sure enough, as we flew the coast we saw about a half a dozen in a clearing in the middle of the willow stand about a mile from the creek where we would land. We circled a few times; they looked up at us as we did. It looked like a few does and a couple bucks. We turned for the beach.

Some beaches on Montague were beautiful tawny colored sand. Others are black sand, but most are rocky slopes exposed by a low tide. The latter was the case with our beach. Not rocks like the ones used to skip across water, but rocks the size of baseballs, footballs and basketballs. It made for a rough and bouncy landing but the cub had what we refer too as "tundra tires," which are similar to big balloons.

After the semi-rough landing, we gathered our gear and started down the beach. Unfortunately the wind was at our backs, which meant by the time we would start into the thicket, the deer would have already scented us. As we approached the willows, we found a small creek giving us a path inward. We discussed it and decided to take our chances with the wind and our scent mainly because the only other way would be to circle around the thicket and crash our way in causing so much noise that it would have defeated the purpose of avoiding the wind. They would have heard us long before they would have smelled us.

With Paul to the right of the creek and me to the left, we began in toward the clearing. Since I had already bagged my tiny little buck across the island, it was Paul's turn at the first shot. As we neared the clearing, I saw a doe jumping towards the thicket. I whispered and pointed: "Paul, Paul, Paul." The doe bounced with each "Paul" and was gone before he ever saw her. He said "What?" I explained what he had missed. He decided to follow the direction I told him the deer went hoping to see her again before the beach. I told him I would double back since deer sometimes circle around in their flight to escape.

I slowly went back down the creek near the opening. As I stepped out of the thicket, I saw some movement on the beach. Right at the high tide mark was a collection of sea debris, seaweed, logs, rope and the like. It gets caught by the flora and creates a kind of barrier sometimes several feet high. This collection was about 18 inches before the beach dropped away a few feet. However, this barrier was brown and round with a pair of white stripes parallel to each other hanging straight down.

"A walrus?" my mind queried, "What's a walrus doing in Prince William Sound?" Walrus don't live anywhere near this part of Alaska. The nearest walrus haul out was Round Island Walrus Sanctuary, but that was in the Bering Sea. The Bering Sea was a few hundred miles and twice across the mainland from here. But standing right there in front of me was a walrus. It swayed to the left, it swayed to the right. Walrus, on land, kind of waddle when they want to move slowly, they lurch when they want to move fast. This was definitely waddling.

I watched in amazement, truly not believing my eyes. I wondered if this would be the first ever documented sighting in Prince William Sound or if there had been others who had lost their way. It was the correct color for a walrus that had been out of the water for a while. It had two white stripes that certainly appeared to be tusks. Then it started to turn toward my right and some strange protrusion appeared out of its left side and behind. I looked and tried to reconcile the two images into one comprehensible form, but it wasn't working. I'm sure I had the expression on my face that a dog has when you make a noise it doesn't understand as I watched.

Then the protrusion began to lift off the ground. As it came up, the lower end of it had a familiar shape to it. The whole form finally began to come into focus and I noticed the familiar shape was the head of a deer, the protrusion began to look like a neck and finally, to round out the transformation the walrus head became a deer's ass and the tusks were the white stripes on the inside of a blacktail's hind legs. My walrus, which was looking to my right, had fully transformed into a doe blacktail looking away and toward my left.

I raised the Marlin to my shoulder, placed the sights on the neck and squeezed the trigger. Boom! The deer bolted to the left as I cycled the lever action. I shot again, boom! She changed direction and ran toward me, I shot again, Bam! She crumpled to the ground kicking. I shot one last time, Kablewy! The deer was still and all was quiet.

I walked over to check on the deer, which had just transformed from a walrus, to confirm she was dead. I set my gun down and took off my pack, pulled out my knife and began skinning. That's the sight Paul saw when he came back out of the thicket and said "What's all the shooting

about?" I said "This doe." He walked up as I took the first hindquarter off. He looked at the carcass and all the wounds and said "God! How many times did you shoot her, you blood thirsty bastard?" There were four wounds, so I guessed "Four times? She was still moving so I had to keep shooting!" I said. He chuckled as he kneeled down to help skin the animal.

We loaded it into our packs and headed back to the plane. It was near 3 p.m. so we took off and headed directly home. The flight back was still a couple hours, so it was dark as we split up the meat, replaced all the wing covers and cowling quilt to head home. Paul denies it, but I swear I could taste a "fishy" taste whenever I ate a meal made with that particular doe.

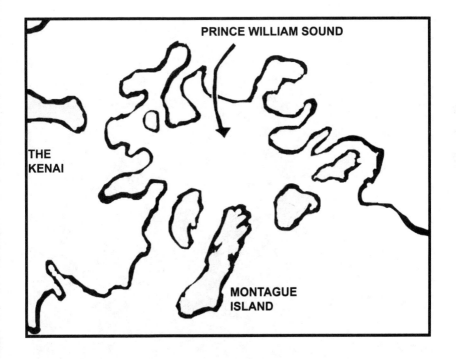

This would be bait for the BIG pike

A Land of World Records

Alaska is a land of world records. Whether it's John Crouse's world record moose taken in 1994, or Harry Swank's Dall sheep in '61, or Roy Lindsley's brown bear from Kodiak in '52, or the world record polar bear taken in '63 by Shelby Longoria. These are not just US records, or even North American records. These are all world records and all taken in Alaska.

The state has given up more than its fair share of record fish, too. Les Anderson's 1985 world record 97 lb. 4 oz. Kenai king salmon, Richard Evan's world record Dolly Varden caught in 1993, Stan Roach's 15 lb. 3 oz. sockeye, not to mention eight-year old David White's 42 lb. 2 oz. rainbow trout caught in '70, which they all thought was a king salmon, it was so big. They are all world records, some of which still stand the test of time. There are other world records in both hunting and fishing which Alaska has given up and some world records that still walk and swim in the state, yet to be taken.

Northern pike, or *Esox lucius*, "water wolf", is a predatory fish which grows fast in the cool of the north. The world record is, depending on your source, currently held in either Germany, IGFA recognized, where Lothar Louis took his record 55 lb. 1 oz. pike from Grefeern Lake, or Czechoslovakia, NFWFHF-recognized, where Jiri Blaha took his 55 lb. 15 oz. monster from the Lipno Reservoir. Either way, neither one is in North America, nor are they Alaskan. That doesn't mean that the world record isn't swimming in Alaska today. This only means that you or someone you know hasn't gone to Alexander Lake, Alaska and cast the right bait into the right spot to crumble all of the above referenced pike world records.

It was one of the first outings of the year and that usually meant pike fishing at Alexander Lake. The salmon wouldn't be in for a few more weeks and this was our early season destination until then. Alexander Lake used to be a great rainbow lake until the pike came in. Some say it was illegal stocking, others claim a flood in the upper Yentna released them from Bulchitna Lake and they spread throughout the Susitna Valley back in the 50's. I frankly didn't care, I was just glad they were here. They made for a fun day of guiding and a fun day of fishing.

Alexander Lake sits at the base of Mount Susitna just a short 30-minute flight by floatplane from Anchorage. The Alaska Department of Fish and Game manages the lake as a "trophy pike" fishery. Elsewhere in Southcentral Alaska, pike have no bag limit, no closed season. You can even spear them, or use a bow to shoot them. Alexander Lake has a slot limit, that is, no bag limit under 22 inches, no retention 22-30 inches, and you can retain only one over 30 inches.

It's a shallow lake and when the sun is warm, its reminiscent of bone fishing on the flats off Florida standing at the bow of the boat with a shooting head on your fly reel. Not that I have ever done that, so I probably don't really know what I am talking about, but it feels like what I watch them do on the fishing shows. I will say that when you get one trailing your top water lure, you can track the wake from 30 feet behind as they stalk your presentation. That's a kick in the pants.

One of my favorite lures to use on a still sunny day, and it was a still sunny day, was a buzz-bait. For the angler who hasn't discovered the old bass standard, let me describe a buzz-bait. It is a firm wire that trails in two ends from the bend to which you tie your leader. One end is a lead headed hook with a rubber or plastic skirt covering the hook. The other trailing end is a large triangle of metal and has offset bends at the two end corners and the whole thing spins on the wire. When the angler retrieves the buzz-bait, the triangle spins like a propeller and planes on the surface quickly. Once it does, this is the desired action, the churning or "buzzing" of the surface. I believe, to the fish, it represents the action of a mouse, a baby duck, or something trying to swim across the surface. Regardless, it drives pike nuts.

I was training a new guide we had hired for the summer season. He had never fished for pike before, but usually, one day on the lake and anybody with even moderate fishing skills could guide a tourist to piscatorial heaven. Lou had moderate fishing skills. We caught the first fish of the day on the first cast of the day and it really stayed that way, almost a fish per cast for about fifteen minutes. I was maneuvering the boat right next to the shore at about five feet from the edge.

The edge was like any other lake edge, generally in a straight line but with little coves and points of smaller sizes. Lou was casting out onto the flats and catching and releasing 12 to 20 inchers, one after the other, and having the time of his life. I had the boat in a good position and decided to cast a few times myself. About half way down the bank, I noticed the cut out little cove, but I, too, was casting out, away from the shore.

I had just released a small pike and turned to set my needle nose pliers back on the bench when I turned and saw movement under the water. From the tiny cut out in the shoreline I saw the pike's head as it slowly swam out underneath our boat. It looked like an alligator with no legs. It had to be at least five feet long because the boat was four feet wide and when the tail finally came into view, the fish was longer than the boat was wide. I pointed to the fish and got Lou's attention. He gasped, "Oh Sh..." Well he said some fairly colorful words to the effect of how large the pike was.

I cast my lure ahead of the fish and buzzed it across its face numerous times. The fish was not in a hurry to leave, but it seemed determined to not be bothered. It disappeared into the lake. Gone.

I was certain that was the only time I would ever see that fish. I went home that night and searched my reference books and found what I had suspected. If that fish truly was sixty inches long, it had to be over sixty pounds at peak weight and that was a new world record. It wasn't just a state record. It wasn't just a North American record. It was the new world record Northern pike. All the books say that the European pike were just genetically superior to those in North America and the record would never be broken unless it was in Europe. Those statements gave me a little patriotic jolt.

Two days later I had a client to take out for pike. We went to Alexander and again, it was a still day. The buzz-bait was the lure of choice; the color was always the same, black skirt with a silver blade. It seemed to be the best combination. I was telling my client of the last trip out here and what I saw. I am not sure he believed me. Guides usually have pretty good whoppers to tell clients, you know. "You should have been here yesterday!" is always a good one.

As we approached the cut out in the bank, I pointed it out to him and as we drifted past, the huge pike shot out again! Right in front of the boat, this time. The guy with me said " Oh my God! That is a five footer. At least!" She was swimming with a little more conviction than the first day I saw her.

As I got home that evening, I called John Carpenter, sports director of Channel 2 news. He was one of my longtime pike fishing buddies. I told him about the fish and asked if he wanted to go do a fishing story and try and catch it. It dawned on me that, like any predator, these big pike were probably territorial and just possibly, this one had staked out that particular cut out as her own season-long lair. It had all the makings of a good lair, deep enough water and just enough area for a big pike to lie in ambush for prey, including smaller pike, to swim by totally unaware that a hungry aggressor was waiting to snatch the lesser fish in its massive jaws with the countless rows of razor-like teeth. He agreed and we planned for Friday - just two more days.

Friday's weather was a day similar to the past two trips I had. Glass smooth water, but it was a bit overcast. It usually doesn't matter as long as the wind isn't blowing. I just do a little better when the sun is baking the water because I think it makes the pike a little more irritable, but overcast was OK too. We began by shooting some footage to set up the story. We mentioned the big one, we referred to her as merely "Lucius", but didn't totally focus on her because we needed to have a fishing report for use on TV either way.

Then we stopped in the channel between the two lobes of Alexander Lake to get footage of random pike. Plus John brought a huge rubber crank bait that looked like a six-inch pike trailing treble hooks that he was just dying to try out. The cameraman John brought along was chuckling, but it worked. We caught some respectable pike on it. Then we headed towards the bank with the hog.

We began drifting the same drift I had set up on the last two trips out to the lake and caught fish after fish after fish. Then I saw the cut out coming. I tried a change in tactics this time. Instead of drifting past the cut out, I rowed out and around the cut out to get a presentation from the opposite side. When the boat was in the appropriate spot, I let go a cast that flew parallel to the bank and landed just about 10 inches from the shore. This retrieve would bring my buzz-bait straight across the opening of the cut out.

Just before my lure hit the water, I began the retrieve. That way the splash and the 'buzz' would be one fluid sound. I tired to emulate a duck landing and beginning to paddle. As the bait began to cross the cut out, there was a large swoosh in the water, a loud and deep plop, and I knew she had come out and taken the bait.

I pulled back on my rod to set the hook. It bent almost back on itself. I told John, "I got a big one!" as the cameraman began to gather his camera gear. The fight was tremendously strong and very violent. Mud was being thrown up from the bottom and I knew the mud was four feet below the water. My arms were pulled on like a strong lab was trying to rip his play-toy from my grasp.

My plan, at least it was my plan last night, was that if I caught her on camera, I was going to get her to the boat, describe that it was a world record and then release her back into the water with the teaser that she would be waiting for viewers whenever they wanted to come to Alexander Lake.

That thought ran through my mind as the tugs at my arm continued and the cameraman was putting the camera to his shoulder. He was just about ready to press the 'record' button when my rod went limp. Nothing! The lake was totally calm.

I let out a very loud guttural yawp. I didn't know what else to do. I knew what had been on the terminal end of my line. I knew I had a professional videographer ready to capture the moment when the good ol' USA took the world record that was never supposed to happen here. I just knew how cool it would have been to show it to the camera, say my rehearsed lines and let it go again.

I didn't know what had gone wrong but I can speculate. Pike have some pretty intimidating teeth. The bigger the pike, the bigger the teeth. When they chomp down on a lure, the teeth lock it in place and I believe, with the really big pike, you have to break some teeth to set the hook. If you don't, when the fish realizes it's not edible, they simply open their mouth and move on. That's how I rationalize the whole event anyway.

I could have let the size shrink over the years as the story sank into memories except that at the time, I sat on the Fish and Game advisory committee and I had told the story to a few biologists from the department. They, of course, dismissed it as a wild fish story for a few weeks and even ribbed me about it for a while. They knew better than I. They were biologists! Then a month or so later, Barry Stratton, one of the biologists who had taken pleasure in the ribbing, came up to me as I was telling some others of the fish and when I finished he said he had spoken with Dave Rutz, the biologist who was in charge of Alexander Lake. He said he told Rutz, "Rydell is trying to claim he missed a 60 inch pike at Alexander!" Rutz had replied, "Probably true. I netted a female right after the spawn three years earlier that measured 58 inches."

The next year the Department of Fish and Game filmed an instructional "Methods and Means of catching Northern Pike" video. They sell it for a modest price on their website and at the headquarters. And they even hired me to be the "open water" instructor in the video presentation.

Alaska. It's a land of world records.

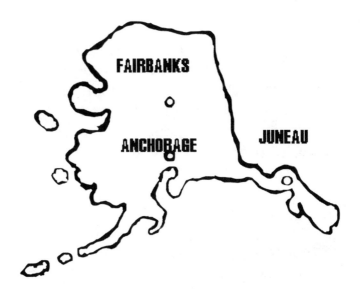

About the author

For over 25 years Rick Rydell has done many things for a living throughout much of Alaska. He has been a guide, a contractor, lead singer in bands, radio talk show host, a project manager at an engineering firm and a host of other occupations, but its easy to see that it has mainly all been to support his outdoors addiction.

He spent his formative years in the Northwest hunting and fishing with family and friends, but like so many others who make the wilderness a part of their lives, at the tender age of 19, he could resist Alaska's call no longer. He packed his belongings, which wasn't much outside a few rods and guns, and moved his life north first to Juneau, then Anchorage, Naknek or anywhere else he could make it.

Rick is a devout family man and lives in Anchorage with his wife Susan, and their children. He is very involved in the community having served on the Fish and Game Advisory Committee, as vice president of both the PTA and his sons' high school football booster club and has mentored kids at the Alaska Military Youth Academy.

You can catch his pontifications each and every weekday morning from 5:30a.m.–9a.m. because he hosts Alaska's most listened to radio talk show on News Radio 650 KENI in Anchorage.